WILEY BLEVINS

CHOOSING AND USING
DECODABLE
TEXTS

Practical Tips and Strategies
for Enhancing Phonics Instruction

SCHOLASTIC
Teacher
RESOURCES

Cover photo © Olivia4567/Shutterstock.

Editor: Maria L. Chang
Cover design by Tannaz Fassihi
Interior design by Maria Lilja
Mini-books illustrated by Abby Carter, Tony Griego, Patrick Girouard, and Jackie Snider

ISBN: 978-1-338-71463-0
Scholastic Inc., 557 Broadway, New York, NY 10012
Copyright © 2021 by Wiley Blevins
Published by Scholastic Inc. All rights reserved.
Printed in the U.S.A.
First printing, January 2021.

6 7 8 9 10   40   30 29 28 27 26 25 24 23

CONTENTS

INTRODUCTION

I walked into the teachers' lounge following my morning of observations. A group of teachers and the school's principal were gathered around the table. As we began to discuss the morning's events, I was struck by the fact that all the teachers had decodable texts in their teaching resource kits, yet none used them. I asked why. No clear reason was offered, and we moved on with our conversation. A few minutes later the principal was called out of the room to take a phone call. It was then that I leaned forward and asked again, "So tell me . . . why aren't you *really* using those decodable texts?" Eyes darted around the room until one teacher finally spoke up and announced, "Because they're boring and stupid."

I was stunned.

I have had conversations with teachers over the years about the importance of children practicing their phonics skills in texts that give them many opportunities to sound out words. "It's in the application where the learning sticks," I always said. And I had spent many years writing decodable texts for publishers. How could anyone hate them this much?

I asked the teachers to show me some of the decodable texts provided with their program. I flipped through a few of them. They were right—boring and stupid. I wondered, "Is this the norm? Are most decodable texts this bad? Is this why children aren't getting enough decoding practice to reach mastery quickly enough in the early elementary grades?" So, I began to search and to question and to study. This book is the result of those efforts.

Let me start by saying that the quality of the materials we use with our students matters. How teachers feel about the materials they are provided also matters. A lot. Give a music teacher a broken piano, and she will never have her students practice playing songs on it. She might teach them about the keys, the middle C position, and so on—but she will never have them play a song because she has an ineffective practice tool. Likewise, if you give a reading teacher problematic teaching tools, these materials will sit in the back of the classroom on a shelf or remain in an unopened box.

But how we teach and the materials we use make a difference—especially with phonics. English is an alphabetic language. We have 26 letters in our alphabet. Alone and in combinations, these letters and spellings stand for the 44 sounds in English. Phonics instruction is the teaching of these spelling-sound correspondences. Learning the basic phonics skills we typically teach in Kindergarten, Grade 1, and Grade 2 gives children a tool to access, or sound out, approximately 84 percent of the words in English text. That's a powerful tool!

Children make the most progress when they apply the phonics skills they learn to their reading and writing every day. Therefore, a decodable text is the key instructional tool needed during phonics instruction to provide ample application opportunities. In this book I explore what decodable texts are, what the research says about them, why they are important for our early readers, and how we can maximize their use in our phonics instruction. I also talk about teachers' attitudes about decodable texts and the reality of what is available—the good, the bad, and the ugly.

Finally, I provide sample high-quality decodable texts and high-impact lesson samples. My hope is that you leave viewing decodable texts through fresh eyes and with renewed possibility.

—WILEY BLEVINS

Bonus Online Materials: The reproducible templates and decodable mini-books in this book are available online. To access these resources, go to **www.scholastic.com/choosingandusingdecodabletexts** and enter your email address and access code: **SC708296**.

CHAPTER 1

WHAT ARE DECODABLE, ACCOUNTABLE TEXTS?

Decodable texts. For some, the term conjures up images of favorite early readers, like *Cat on the Mat* by Brian Wildsmith or *Hop on Pop* by Dr. Seuss. For others, it induces shivers and scowls. So, what are decodable texts and how do they differ from other kinds of texts we have in our classrooms? A **decodable text** is a story or book that is controlled based on the phonics skills taught up to that point in the scope and sequence, with an emphasis on the new target skill for that instructional cycle (e.g., week of instruction). That is, the majority of the words in a decodable text can be sounded out based on the sound–spelling relationships children have learned—giving them loads of opportunities to apply those skills to real reading experiences.

For example, if a teacher is teaching Long *a* spelled *ai* and *ay,* her students might read a book called *Spain in May.* This book would contain a lot of words with *ai* and *ay,* as well as words with previously taught phonics skills. It would also contain some irregular high-frequency words—words such as *they, some,* and *was*—that had already been taught. It might even contain a couple of story words, such as *river,* that would be neither decodable (yet) nor high-frequency words already taught (although these would be minimal and might not exist at all).

Since the goal of phonics instruction is to develop students' ability to read connected text independently, decodable text (which I also call *accountable text*) at the beginning level of reading instruction helps children develop a sense of comfort in and control over their reading growth. The tight connection between what children learn in phonics and what they read is essential for building a faster foundation in early reading. These texts should be a key and daily learning tool in early phonics instruction. These accountable (phonics-based) texts need to be reread to build fluency, discussed to develop comprehension, and written about to provide opportunities for children to apply and transfer their growing phonics skills to writing.

Take a look at the two texts below. Let's say the children are learning Short *i.* They have already learned Short *a* and all the consonants. What do you notice? The leveled text has a pattern and far fewer Short-*i* words to practice decoding.

The decodable text breaks the pattern and has many more words with Short *i*—the target phonics skill. With which text will children get more practice with Short *i*? Which text will get them to mastery faster? Which text more closely matches what they have been taught? The decodable text, of course!

Leveled Text

Decodable Text

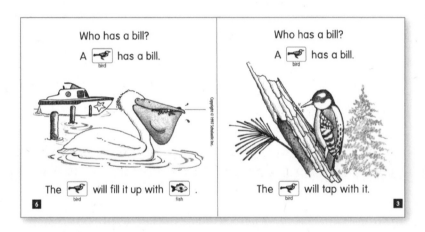

TYPES OF TEXT IN PRIMARY-GRADE CLASSROOMS

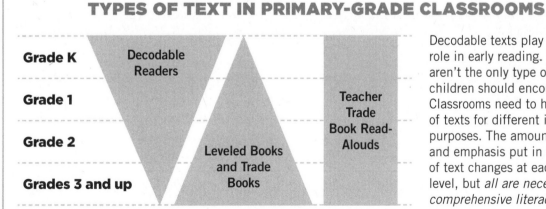

Decodable texts play a primary role in early reading. But they aren't the only type of texts children should encounter. Classrooms need to have a variety of texts for different instructional purposes. The amount of time and emphasis put in each type of text changes at each grade level, but *all are necessary for a comprehensive literacy solution.*

Two States: Different Decodable Text Requirements

Several departments of education have defined *decodable texts* for their states. This began around 2000 when California and Texas, the two states that dominate textbook creation in the United States, required the inclusion of decodable texts in their state reading adoptions. As you will read, their definitions vary and have evolved over time.

In the English Language Arts/English Language Development Framework for California Public Schools, it says:

> "[D]ecodable texts are books and other reading materials that consist of words learned by sight (such as irregularly spelled high-frequency words) and, importantly and most prominently, words that consist of regular letter-sound and spelling-sound correspondences, especially those that children have already learned. Specifically, decodable texts are reading materials designed to prompt beginning readers to apply their increasing knowledge of phonics and practice full alphabetic decoding to identify words. In decodable texts, 75 to 80 percent of words consist solely of previously taught letter-sound and spelling-sound correspondences and the remaining 20 to 25 percent of the words are previously taught high-frequency irregularly spelled words and story or content words. The value of the decodable texts is time limited but significant for beginning readers. These materials provide children the opportunity to apply and practice what they're learning about the alphabetic code, which enhances their reading acquisition. . . . The amount of time devoted to decodable texts depends on how quickly children grasp the code and develop automaticity. Some children need considerable practice with the decodable texts. Others need less practice with decodable texts. Instruction, therefore, is differentiated."

In "Decodable Texts for Beginning Reading Instruction: The Year 2000 Basals," Hoffman and his colleagues summarize the Texas requirements for decodable texts as part of their 2000 state reading adoption. They state:

> "Originally . . . an average of 51 percent of the words in each selection should be decodable in those selections [a] publisher had designated as decodable. The percentage of 51 percent was drawn literally from the Texas Essential Knowledge and Skills (TEKS) requirement that a majority of words be decodable. Later, the State Board of Education raised the standard to 80 percent of the words for each selection deemed decodable by the publisher. The rationale for an 80-percent level of decodability was not tied to any research evidence."

This decodability requirement still exists today in Texas and controls the creation of decodable texts nationwide.

WHY ARE DECODABLE TEXTS AN ESSENTIAL LEARNING TOOL?

Children progress at a much faster rate in phonics when the bulk of instructional time is spent on applying the skills to authentic reading and writing experiences, rather than isolated skill-and-drill work. At least half of a phonics lesson should be devoted to application exercises. It's in the application where the learning sticks. Decodable texts provide this application.

The chart below details the impact more time spent reading and writing about decodable texts can have on children's progress in phonics. It shows two teachers I observed at the same school (on the same day) and illustrates the cumulative effect of application time. It is representative of a larger issue with phonics instruction and the distribution of high-impact activities during the limited time spent on this instruction during a typical reading block.

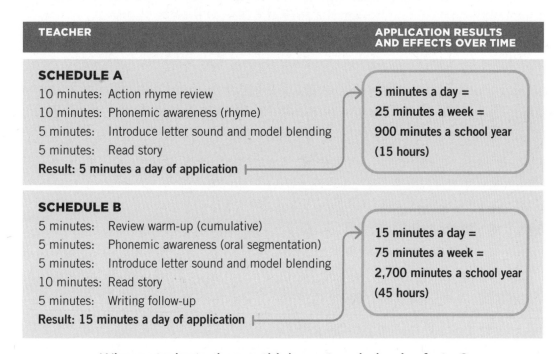

TEACHER	APPLICATION RESULTS AND EFFECTS OVER TIME
SCHEDULE A 10 minutes: Action rhyme review 10 minutes: Phonemic awareness (rhyme) 5 minutes: Introduce letter sound and model blending 5 minutes: Read story **Result: 5 minutes a day of application**	**5 minutes a day =** **25 minutes a week =** **900 minutes a school year** **(15 hours)**
SCHEDULE B 5 minutes: Review warm-up (cumulative) 5 minutes: Phonemic awareness (oral segmentation) 5 minutes: Introduce letter sound and model blending 10 minutes: Read story 5 minutes: Writing follow-up **Result: 15 minutes a day of application**	**15 minutes a day =** **75 minutes a week =** **2,700 minutes a school year** **(45 hours)**

Whose students do you think mastered phonics faster?

Why is decodable, accountable text so important for use in Kindergarten and Grade 1 phonics instruction? Juel and Roper-Schneider explained this in their 1985 study. Note that when they conducted their study, formal reading instruction began in Grade 1, not Kindergarten (like today).

> "The selection of text used very early in first grade may, at least in part, determine the strategies and cues children learn to use, and persist in using, in subsequent word identification. . . . In particular, emphasis on a phonics method seems to make little sense if children are given initial texts to read where the words do not follow regular letter-sound correspondence generalizations. . . . [T]he types of words which appear in beginning reading texts may well exert a more powerful influence in shaping children's word-identification strategies than the method of reading instruction."

On the next page are two texts that illustrate this concept. Let's say children have learned consonants, Short *a,* Short *i,* and high-frequency words such as *the, on, are.* How are children accessing the words in each text? Now, consider the cumulative effect this would have on how children approach other texts when first learning to read.

If using initial letter and picture clues is easier and works most of the time in the simple, patterned books children are reading (e.g., in Levels A to D), then that is what they will think reading is primarily and will attack each new text in this way—scanning the illustrations before reading the text, relying on the pattern, and using partial word clues. But what happens in later levels when the direct connection between the text and pictures isn't as strong and those clues stop working? How easy will it be for these children to change the way they approach text to read it? How easy will it be to break this unreliable and bad habit?

In contrast, children who read decodable texts learn the utility of their phonics skills right away through this consistent application. They focus first on the letters and spellings in the words on the page. This reading strategy works the majority of the time and is (and always will be) reliable. Children only need to use other ways to attack words for those *few* words that are irregular or contain unknown sound-spellings.

TYPE OF TEXT	TEXT SAMPLE (LEVEL C)	HOW STUDENTS ACCESS WORDS
Patterned Text	 Puppies get into lots of silly spots. 2 puppies (are) <u>in</u> (the) boots.  Puppies get into lots of silly spots. 2 puppies (are) <u>in</u> (the) flowers.	**Underlined words** = decodable words based on taught phonics skills **Circled words** = high-frequency words previously learned **All other words** = initial letter and picture clues, then guessing With this kind of text, children learn the pattern and rely primarily on memorizing high-frequency words and using picture clues to read the text. When they pick up a new text their eyes generally go first to the illustrations, then to the words on the page.
Decodable Text	 <u>Can Sam sit?</u> <u>Sam can sit in</u> (the) <u>chair.</u>  <u>Can</u> (the) <u>cat sit?</u> (The) <u>cat can sit.</u> <u>It sits</u> (on)(the) <u>mat.</u>	**Underlined words** = decodable words based on taught phonics skills **Circled words** = high-frequency words previously learned **All other words** = initial letter and picture clues, then guessing With this kind of text, children sound out the majority of the words. The other words are learned high-frequency words, except *chair*. This word can be determined from the picture clue and makes the story more natural-sounding and interesting.

Brain Research on Early Text Impact

Cognitive scientists have been able to show evidence through the use of functional MRI imaging (brain pictures) why text selection for beginning readers has such an impact on reading development. A groundbreaking 2015 brain research study out of Stanford taught the participants one of two ways to read a new alphabetic text: sounding out the words using phonics or learning words by sight as whole units. What did the scientists find when they looked at the functional MRI images? The participants who read by sounding out words activated the parts of the brain that skilled readers use to access text. What about those readers who were taught to read by memorizing words by sight as whole units? Their brains behaved in the same way as the brains of unskilled readers. That is, it was as if this type of reading was wiring their brains to access words in a less-efficient way.

It is important to note that the participants who learned by sight words got off to a faster start. But that learning was not transferable to new, unknown words, and they hit a wall. The participants who learned to sound out words got off to a slower start. It was work. Sometimes hard work. But that learning transferred to new, unknown words, and those readers were able to surpass the sight-word readers.

This is often the difference I observe with children in Kindergarten who start learning to read using patterned, leveled texts as opposed to those who learn reading decodable texts. Generally, most of these patterned, leveled-text readers take off fast and with relative ease and don't "hit a wall" until sometime in Grade 1 because they are quite skilled at memorizing the words in these simple leveled books. It gives their teachers a false sense of reading growth. In addition, districts often require teachers to send their students on to Grade 1 with a "level" designation (e.g., Level E), but without conducting any mastery assessment of Kindergarten phonics skills to see if there are foundational-skill needs. This leaves the Grade 1 teachers at a disadvantage in meeting these students' needs early in the school year to address foundational-skill holes. A level designation doesn't tell you much information about phonics-skill mastery since leveled books aren't created using phonics as a criteria.

Characteristics of Strong Phonics Instruction

There are seven characteristics of strong phonics instruction (listed below). For years I have worked with teachers and publishers to ensure that these were in place in their foundational-skills instruction. You will notice that one of these characteristics is the reading of connected texts—decodable, accountable stories. Therefore, these texts are an essential part of phonics instruction.

1 Readiness Skills
Phonemic awareness and alphabet recognition are the two best predictors of early reading success. These skills play a key role in foundational-skill instruction and in getting children ready to decode (read by sounding out) and encode (write/spell) words.

2 Scope and Sequence
While there is no "right" phonics scope and sequence, there are those that are more beneficial for student learning. These scopes and sequences start with high-utility vowels and consonants so words can be formed as early as possible. They separate confusing letters and sounds. They also have a built-in review and repetition cycle to ensure mastery. A strong scope and sequence serves as the spine of all the instruction and is tightly linked to the stories children read.

3 Blending
This is the primary decoding strategy, in which children string together the sounds in a printed word to read it. This strategy must be frequently modeled and applied in connected text reading.

4 Dictation
This is guided spelling. It is a critical way for teachers to think aloud about how they write words as they model for children how to use and transfer their phonics skills to written words, sentences, and stories. Weekly dictation is not a test, rather a guided exercise that can help accelerate children's use of phonics skills in writing. It should begin in early Kindergarten (e.g., teacher says a sound and children write the letter, then proceed to writing simple words and a simple sentence) and progress in complexity throughout the grades. Dictation exercises should include words with the new target phonics skill as well as words with previously taught skills to extend the learning and supported application.

5 Word-Awareness Activities
Word-building and word sorts are two ways to increase children's awareness of how English words work. These activities involve conversations and observations about words, ensuring that the phonics instruction is active,

engaging, and thought-provoking—the goal of strong phonics instruction. These activities can help consolidate and solidify student learning.

6 High-Frequency Words

High-frequency words are the most common words in English, but some of these words are irregular. That means they can't be sounded out using the standard phonics skills we teach in Grades K–2. These words need to be taught differently. Research-based routines, such as the Read/Spell/Write/Extend routine (page 39), can accelerate student learning of these words. Children need to focus on the individual sounds and spellings of these words—highlighting the "irregular" part—to orthographically map the words so they can be readily accessed while reading and writing.

7 Reading Connected Text

Using controlled, decodable text at the beginning of reading instruction helps children develop a sense of control and comfort in their reading. The application of the phonics skills to authentic reading experiences is critical for mastery and transfer. Reading these texts should be followed by writing to give children a direct and scaffolded opportunity to apply the phonics skill in encoding and documenting understanding.

Plus . . . You, the Teacher

The success of all these characteristics rests on the shoulders of a highly trained teacher. In addition, a teacher's attitudes and background knowledge or phonics expertise play a crucial role in instructional success.

Common Causes of Phonics Instructional Failure

Having the seven characteristics of phonics instruction, including the use of decodable texts, in place isn't enough. There are some common obstacles teachers may face when delivering phonics instruction that can impede or limit student learning. Below, I list ten of the most common causes of phonics instructional failure based on my research and classroom practice. Notice that causes 2 and 3 are directly related to the use of decodable texts.

1 Inadequate or Nonexistent Review and Repetition Cycle

We underestimate the amount of time it takes young learners to master phonics skills. When we introduce a new skill, we should systematically and purposefully review it for the next four to six weeks. Our goal must be to teach to mastery rather than just exposure. With the fast pacing of most curricula, a more substantial review and repetition cycle often must be added.

Look at the skill you are teaching this week, then mark all the instances you review it in the upcoming four to six weeks, including in the texts children read (note the variety of words used). Increase opportunities to practice through additional words in blending work, dictation, and repeated readings of previously read decodable stories.

2 Lack of Application to Real Reading and Writing Experiences

Children progress at a much faster rate in phonics when the bulk of instructional time is spent on applying the skills to authentic reading and writing experiences, rather than isolated skill-and-drill work. At least 50 percent of a phonics lesson should be devoted to application exercises. Evaluate the average amount of time your students spend on reading and writing during your phonics lessons.

3 Inappropriate Reading Materials to Practice Skills

The connection between what we teach and what we have young learners read has a powerful effect on their word-reading strategies and their phonics and spelling skills. It also affects their motivation to read. Examine a few pages from the books you give your students to read in K–1. Children should be able to sound out more than 50 percent of these words based on the phonics skills you have taught them up to that point. If not, you need to provide more controlled text until they get additional phonics skills under their belts and develop a sense of comfort and control in their reading abilities. You can usually transition to more challenging texts in the second half of Grade 1. Reading decodable texts should be a daily phonics lesson activity.

4 Ineffective Use of the Gradual Release Model

Teachers of struggling readers often spend too much of the instructional time doing the "heavy lifting," such as over-modeling and having children simply repeat. Whoever does the thinking in a lesson, does the learning. Children might struggle, but you are there to provide corrective feedback and support. Limit "parrot" activities in which children simply repeat what they hear or see.

5 Too Much Time Lost During Transitions

Phonics lessons often require a lot of manipulatives and materials. Turn transitional times, when materials are distributed or collected, into valuable instructional moments by reviewing skills (e.g., singing the ABC song, doing a phonemic-awareness task, reviewing sound-letter action rhymes to focus children's attention on an instructional goal). To maximize impact, plan these transitions at the beginning of the week (e.g., select three or four great transitions per week) around skills you want to review.

6 Limited Teacher Knowledge of Research-Based Phonics Routines and Linguistics

Teachers with backgrounds in phonics or linguistics are better equipped to make meaningful instructional decisions, analyze student errors, and improve the language and delivery of instruction. Also, teacher attitudes toward phonics instructional materials (e.g., decodable text) and routines (e.g., sorts, word-building, blending) matter. Explore these within grade-level teams.

7 Inappropriate Pacing of Lessons

Teachers often spend too much time on activities they enjoy or are easier for children and less time on the more challenging or "meaty" activities that increase learning. High-impact activities include blending, dictation, word-building, word sorts, and reading and writing about decodable texts. Keep lessons fast paced and rigorous. Phonics should be fun, with children active and engaged throughout the entire lesson. The bulk of time should be devoted to real reading and writing experiences.

8 No Comprehensive or Cumulative Mastery Assessment Tools

Teachers should assess phonics skills over an extended period of time to ensure mastery. Weekly assessments focusing on one skill often give "false positives." That is, they show movement toward learning, but not mastery. If the skill isn't worked on enough for subsequent weeks, learning can decay. Cumulative assessments help you determine which skills children have truly mastered. Comprehensive assessments help you place children along a phonics continuum (for targeted small-group instruction to meet their needs) and can be used to determine whether or not children have met phonics grade-level expectations.

9 Transitioning to Multisyllabic Words Too Late

Most curricula focus on one-syllable words too long in Grade 2, yet the stories children read at that grade are filled with more challenging, multisyllabic words. More emphasis needs to be given to transitioning to longer words at this grade (e.g., going from known to new words, like *can/candle*, and teaching the six major syllable types [closed, open, *r*-controlled, vowel team, vowel–silent *e*, consonant + *le*]). Add this to your weekly lessons all year.

10 Overdoing It (Especially Isolated Skill Work)

Some curricula overemphasize phonics (especially the isolated skill type of work), while ignoring other key aspects of early reading needs (e.g., vocabulary and background knowledge-building) that are essential to long-term reading progress. Modify your reading time to provide better balance.

The Research on Decodable Text: A Snapshot

In addition to my research on decodable texts, other researchers have examined this critical instructional tool. While there is surprisingly little research on decodable texts, what *has* been done highlights its impact on phonics learning. The research also points to areas in need of further exploration.

Below is a summary of the key research studies on decodable texts. I also provide a more in-depth look at my 2000 study in the following pages.

RESEARCH STUDY	SUMMARY	DISCUSSION
Juel and Roper-Schneider (1985) *Reading Research Quarterly*	"The selection of text used very early in first grade may, at least in part, determine the strategies and cues children learn to use, and persist in using, in subsequent word identification. . . . In particular, emphasis on a phonics method seems to make little sense if children are given initial texts to read where the words do not follow regular letter-sound correspondence generalizations. . . . [T]he types of words which appear in beginning reading texts may well exert a more powerful influence in shaping children's word identification strategies than the method of reading instruction."	The texts we use in phonics lessons have a powerful effect on how children attack words while reading. In essence, the words determine how children must access them. Using decodable texts encourages the sounding out of words, which is a more reliable strategy than using picture or context clues and guessing.
Blevins (2000) *Phonics From A to Z*	"This study examined the role of decodable text in early reading instruction and its importance in decoding, spelling, and reading motivation for young learners. A study of U.S. first graders showed the experimental group (decodable-text readers) significantly outperformed students in a control group (patterned-book readers) on the Woodcock Reading Mastery Test, decoding transfer test, spelling test, and reading attitudes survey."	See pages 20–25 for details on my 2000 study.
Mesmer (2005) *Reading & Writing Quarterly*	"Treatment participants reading highly decodable text were found to apply letter/sound knowledge a greater extent than control participants. They also were more accurate and relied on examiners less for assistance."	Decodable texts increase children's phonics-application opportunities, which can lead to greater decoding accuracy.

RESEARCH STUDY	SUMMARY	DISCUSSION
Jenkins, Peyton, Sanders, Vadasy (2004) *Scientific Studies of Reading*	"At-risk 1st graders were randomly assigned to tutoring in more or less decodable texts, and instruction in the same phonics program. . . . A control group did not receive tutoring in phonics or story reading. Both tutored groups significantly surpassed the control on an array of decoding, word reading, passage reading, and comprehension measures. However, the more and less decodable text groups did not differ on any posttest."	This study is often used to question the potential benefits of decodable texts over other readers. The big issue with that conclusion is that this study was conducted on children who received phonics instruction, including decodable-text reading during Tier 1 instruction in their classrooms, then were pulled out for additional instruction in an intervention setting—some with highly controlled text for phonics and some with little control for phonics. Some children received a double dose of decodable texts. This study does NOT discuss the impact of decodable readers on Tier 1 instruction, which other studies have shown to be beneficial. What this study did, however, is raise some important questions. The children who read the "more decodable texts" read from texts that I would classify as weaker in terms of comprehensibility (stilted language and less frequent vocabulary, as in: *Dot had a bag. The bag had a tag.*). The children who read from the "less decodable texts" read stories with more natural-sounding text and filled with important high-frequency words (e.g., *I go up the steps. You go up the steps. I go into the house. You go into the house.*). This raises the issue of the quality of the decodable texts and its impact. It also hints at the need for early reading texts to include multiple exposures to words and ample practice with the most frequently used words in English, which has more immediate impact on children's reading of texts over the less-frequent words in the decodable texts used in the study.
Cheathem and Allor (2012) *Reading and Writing*	"Collectively the results indicate that decodability is a critical characteristic of early reading text as it increases the likelihood that students will use a decoding strategy and results in immediate benefits, particularly with regard to accuracy. The study points to the need for multiple-criteria text with decodability being one characteristic in ensuring that students develop the alphabetic principle that is necessary for successful reading, rather than text developed based on the single criterion of decodability."	Decodable texts increase children's decoding practice because so many words can be sounded out. However, early reading texts should not be completely (100 percent) decodable as that is not the only criteria for making a strong early reading text.

RESEARCH STUDY	SUMMARY	DISCUSSION
Chu and Chen (2014) *Psychological Reports*	"Empirical evidence shows that explicit phonics teaching is beneficial for English word reading. However, there has been controversy as to whether phonics teaching should incorporate meaning-involved decodable text instruction to facilitate children's word reading. This study compares the effects of phonics teaching with and without decodable text instruction on immediate and delayed English word reading in 117 Taiwanese children learning English . . . the Phonics+ group (using the decodable texts) performed better . . . (This) indicated that incorporated meaning-involved decodable text reading might offer another better facilitative linking route for English word reading."	This study examined the positive effects of adding decodable texts to phonics lessons for children learning English as a second or additional language.
Frey (2012) (dissertation)	"High-performing readers began the year reading beyond the level of the decodable texts and interacted with the decodable texts minimally. Mid-performing students clearly benefited from reading the decodable texts . . . For struggling readers, however, the decodable texts were too difficult and consistently low accuracy and low fluency scores were coupled with a range of problematic reading behaviors that demonstrated the disproportionate difficulty struggling readers had with the decodable texts."	This study supported the benefits of decodable readers for on-level students. However, it noted difficulties below-level students had with these texts due to (1) the fact that these children hadn't mastered previous phonics skills but were expected to keep up with the grade-level pace, and (2) the poor quality of the texts, including the repeated inclusion of low-frequency words and the lack of repetition across texts. The study also noted the "non-linear" increase in difficulty in these texts in the second half of Grade 1, where multiple spellings are introduced for one sound at a rapid pace and how challenging that was for the struggling (below-level) readers. This study highlights the importance of differentiating phonics instruction, including the use of decodable texts, and the need to scaffold the reading of these texts for struggling readers.

Decodable Text—Does It Really Matter?

In 2000, I conducted a study to examine the effectiveness of decodable text in promoting word-identification skills, phonics, and spelling abilities, as well as positive reading attitudes in early readers. Previous research on the influence of basal readers had indicated that the types of words that appear in beginning reading texts exert a powerful influence in shaping children's word-identification strategies (Juel & Roper-Schneider, 1985). However, there had been no research on the direct effects of decodable texts on early reading growth. In my study, I hypothesized that children who receive reading practice with decodable (controlled) text would achieve great mastery in early reading skills than children who continued reading with standard classroom trade literature as follow-up reading to phonics instruction. I defined *decodable text* as text in which the vocabulary is controlled based on knowledge of previously taught sound-spelling relationships. *Trade literature* refers to books with a variety of genres and formats designed for children to build their vocabularies and read independently. These trade books are not controlled for phonic elements.

RESEARCH QUESTIONS

My research questions included:

- Does practice with decodable text in conjunction with a systematic phonics program accelerate word-identification skills for first-grade students?

- Do first graders who use decodable text demonstrate significantly greater gains in word-identification skills than a comparison group of students who use trade literature?

SAMPLE

Two New York City public schools participated in my study from September 1999 to February 2000. There were two first-grade classrooms selected at each school—one experimental classroom using decodable text and one control classroom using trade literature. A total of 101 children in first grade participated in this research. The selected schools were in the lowest third of the district, based on achievement scores. Ninety percent of the students in this district qualify for free or reduced lunch, and 80 percent were identified as Latino. Sixty-two percent of the students were classified as below grade level. Both schools used the same systematic and explicit phonics instruction covering the identical phonics scope and sequence. The only difference between the experimental and control classrooms was the type of text used for reading practice: the decodable text or the standard trade literature series.

PROGRAM BACKGROUND

The decodable texts used in the study were written to directly address the requirements outlined in *Becoming a Nation of Readers* (Anderson, Hiebert, Scott & Wilkinson, 1985).

Students in both groups read a major piece of literature for the first week and received phonics lessons follow-up practice five days a week. First graders in the experimental group practiced reading with decodable (controlled) text for their phonics lessons follow-up. The controlled texts were 100 percent controlled for phonics and sight words (for example: *Sam sat. Sam sat in the sand. Sam sat and sat.*). The major reading text was 80 percent controlled for phonics and sight words, as well as being specially written and illustrated.

In comparison, the control group's phonics lessons follow-up included patterned and predictable text (for example: *Sam sees a sandwich. Sam sees a snake. Sam sees a sailor. Sam sees a lot!*). For its major reading text, the control group used popular first-grade books written by well-known authors. Many of these texts were approximately 35 percent decodable.

Controlled-text percentages were determined through a decodability analysis I did based on a clear scope and sequence of phonics skills. In addition, a review of Marcy Stein's pivotal study "Analyzing Beginning Reading Programs: The Relationship Between Decoding Instruction and Text" (Stein, Johnson & Gutlohn, 1999) confirmed controlled-text percentages for both the experimental and control groups of children.

PROFESSIONAL DEVELOPMENT

I conducted an initial training session with the experimental-group teachers on how to incorporate the decodable text into their comprehensive reading program. Each participating classroom was visited and observed four days per week—two days by me and two days by my research assistant. This method ensured that all teachers stayed on pace, taught the phonics lessons as intended, and read the required books. We kept detailed anecdotal notes of these sessions. In addition, we formally observed each classroom for two weeks to develop classroom profiles.

ASSESSMENT MEASURES

This study included the following four assessment measures.

- **The Woodcock Reading Mastery Test (WRMT)–Word Identification Sub-Test:** Required children to look at printed words and read them aloud.

- **The Blevins Phonics-Phonemic Awareness Quick Assessment:** A simple, five-word spelling test administered at the start of school. Students fall into three categories—below level, on level, and above level. This test quickly identifies children in need of intervention and provides information about children's phonemic awareness and phonics proficiency.

- **Decoding Assessment:** A phonics mastery assessment developed specifically for the study. It consisted of 20 words, all decodable based on the phonics scope and sequence. Ten of the words presented on the assessment appeared multiple times (four or more) in the reading selections read by both groups of children. The other ten words never appeared in the stories read by both groups, or they appeared only once. Ability to decode 75 percent of the words or more was necessary to receive a "passing" score.

- **Reading Attitudes Survey:** An informal interview-style assessment, which evaluates how children feel about learning to read, as well as how they perceive themselves as readers.

This study included a pre- and post-test design for the WRMT, the Blevins Phonics-Phonemic Awareness Quick Assessment, and the Reading Attitudes Survey. Pretesting was conducted in September 1999, and posttesting was conducted in February 2000. The Decoding Assessment was administered only at the end of the study, in February 2000.

DATA ANALYSIS

WRMT–Word Identification Sub-Test Results

Results revealed that children in the experimental group significantly outperformed children in the control group on the WRMT. Analysis determined that W-score differences were statistically significant at $F(1.69)=12.954$, $p<.001$. The effect size was determined to be ES=.16. (See graph below.)

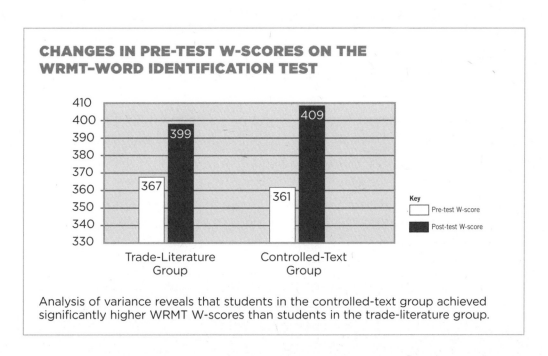

CHANGES IN PRE-TEST W-SCORES ON THE WRMT–WORD IDENTIFICATION TEST

Key
☐ Pre-test W-score
■ Post-test W-score

Analysis of variance reveals that students in the controlled-text group achieved significantly higher WRMT W-scores than students in the trade-literature group.

Furthermore, results revealed that a significantly greater number of children using the decodable text for their reading practice achieved on-level WRMT mastery: 72 percent decodable-text students vs. 54 percent trade-literature students. The controlled-text group made a significant leap from 28 percent on-level mastery at the beginning of the year to 72 percent mastery in February. In contrast, the trade-literature group only increased WRMT on-level mastery from 40 percent in September to 54 percent in February. Some children in the controlled-text group achieved as much as two years' growth in one-half year. The average student growth for this group was one year of growth during one-half year of school.

Phonics-Phonemic Awareness Quick Assessment Results

Findings revealed that a significantly greater number of decodable-text students vs. trade-literature students achieved mastery on the Phonics-Phonemic Awareness Quick Assessment: 92 percent decodable-text students vs. 66 percent trade-literature students. Ninety-two percent of controlled-text students were able to spell all five words correctly.

Decoding (Phonics Mastery) Assessment Results

Results revealed that 87 percent of the children using the decodable text achieved mastery (75 percent or higher score) on the Decoding Assessment, as compared with only 54 percent of the children in the trade-literature group.

Reading Attitudes Survey Results

Findings showed that significantly fewer children reading decodable text vs. trade literature reported a dislike of reading or identified themselves as poor readers. Only 3 percent of decodable-text students reported that they didn't enjoy reading vs. 11 percent of trade-literature students. The percentage of children in the controlled-text group who reported a dislike of reading decreased during the study, from 14 percent in September to only 3 percent in February. I attribute this to their growing sense of confidence and control in their reading. In comparison, the percentage of children in the trade-literature group who reported a dislike of reading actually increased during the study, from 6 percent in September to 11 percent in February.

Classroom Observation Results

Classroom observations indicated that working with controlled/decodable text carried over to other important areas of teaching, such as read-aloud modeling and writing activities. In general, we observed over time that teachers paid more attention to words and specifically how words work.

As further evidence of the power of controlled text, classroom observations also revealed that children in the controlled-text group were more confident in tackling difficult books for their at-home reading choices. It was observed that children in the experimental group would examine the words in books before selecting a story to take home. Conversely, children in the control group were observed to have difficulty in choosing books with appropriate text for their reading level.

DISCUSSION

Overall, children in the controlled-text group were more prepared to transfer their phonics skills to new words presented to them in formal assessments. In addition, these results reinforce what previous research by motivation experts has shown: Reading success breeds reading self-confidence and enjoyment of reading. This study also reinforces that the type of text for beginning readers does matter. Children who use decodable/controlled text in their early reading instruction get off to a stronger start in their reading development.

But I Use Leveled Books . . . How Do I Include Decodable Texts in My Instruction?

What do you do if you want to include decodable texts in your phonics instruction, but are using a guided reading, leveled-book approach in your reading program? Teachers I work with have taken my Guided Reading Phonics Scope and Sequence (pages 26–27) and layered on a set of strong decodable readers. They use these readers at each level to focus on the target phonics skills listed for that level. When reading other books with children, such as the leveled books in their book rooms, these teachers highlight words with the target phonics skills and include follow-up reading and writing activities (e.g., dictation and word-building) connected to those phonics skills. In addition, they evaluate children's use of these skills in their writing and reinforce them. This ensures there is an increased amount of decodable-text reading at each level and there is more focus on a targeted set of phonics skills at that level.

Use the chart on the following pages to create your own Guided Reading/ Decodable Text planning chart.

Guided Reading Phonics Scope and Sequence

GUIDED READING LEVEL	RECOMMENDED PHONICS SKILL	NOTES	MY DECODABLE READERS
A	**Alphabet** (Basic letter sounds and introducing the alphabet principle)	Children read patterned text to learn concepts of print and some basic high-utility sight words, such as *I, can, see*.	
B	**Alphabet** (Basic letter sounds, highlighting awareness of short-vowel sounds and securing knowledge of all consonant sounds)	Children read patterned text, but the phonics instruction includes the reading of simple 2- and 3-letter short-vowel words with blending.	
C	**Alphabet** (Basic letter sounds and emphasizing the concept of blending sounds to read words using one or more short vowels)	Children read patterned text with some short-vowel VC and CVC words.	
D	**Short vowels *a, i*** (Full blending and mastery are expected from here on)	Children begin reading texts that contain larger numbers of decodable words. Instruction can also include inflectional endings, consonant blends, and plurals.	
E	**Short vowels *o, u, e***	Instruction can also include consonant digraphs.	

GUIDED READING LEVEL	RECOMMENDED PHONICS SKILL	NOTES	MY DECODABLE READERS
F	**Final *e*** (Use minimal contrasts to help children grasp the new concept: *hat/hate*)	Reinforce consonant blends and consonant digraphs.	
G	**Long vowels *a, e*** (Multiple spelling from here on)	Contrast short- and long-vowel sounds.	
H	**Long vowels *o, i, u***	Instruction can also focus on introducing simple multisyllabic words.	
I	***r*-controlled vowels *er, ir, ur, ar, or, ore*** **Diphthongs** *oi, oy, ou, ow* **Variant vowels** *oo, au, aw*	Instruction can also focus on introducing simple multisyllabic words (e.g., words with inflectional endings, simple prefixes, compound words).	
J–M	**Two- and three-syllable words**	Review one-syllable words with short vowels, final *e*, long vowels, complex vowels, diphthongs, and *r*-controlled vowels to ensure mastery.	

WHAT DISTINGUISHES STRONG FROM WEAK DECODABLE TEXTS?

Not all decodable texts are created equal.

We've all seen decodable texts of a lesser quality. Texts with poor illustrations. Texts with sentences that were tongue twisters or didn't quite make sense. Texts we feared our students wouldn't enjoy or be able to easily comprehend. It's one of the reasons some teachers dislike this critical instructional tool so much. Yet, while some publishers have unfortunately created weak decodable texts, the standard for decodable texts has always been high in the research.

In 1985, the government document *Becoming a Nation of Readers* (Anderson, et al) provided a set of criteria for creating controlled, decodable text. According to the report, this type of text should include the following three criteria:

1. Comprehensible: The stories should make sense and follow natural-sounding English spoken and written patterns. No sentences should be in these stories that you, as a proficient speaker and reader of English, have not uttered, written, or read. Vocabulary must be understandable. Words must be derived primarily from children's speaking and listening vocabularies.

2. Instructive: The majority* of the words must be decodable based on the sound spellings previously taught. In addition, there should be enough words with the new, target phonics skill for children to get ample practice decoding words with that skill. There must be a strong connection between instruction and text.

* Note: Research has NEVER given a percentage of decodability, and sources that require or claim a decodability requirement (e.g., 80 percent or 90 percent) have arbitrarily decided on their definition of *majority*. This has directly resulted in the creation of weaker decodable texts, as the percentage of decodability became the driver of the creation of these texts, rather than a balance of all three criteria.

3. Engaging: These connected, decodable texts must be engaging enough for children to want to read them again and again. Children need to revisit these texts to develop fluency and increase reading rate. The texts should also be worth writing and talking about. In early texts, some of the engagement and discussion will be derived from the high-quality photos and illustrations, but the text must support them.

I've written and helped publish hundreds of these decodable books throughout my career, so it came as quite a surprise when teachers told me how much they disliked this type of text. Curious, I began to explore decodable texts widely available from educational and trade publishers. Many of these texts appeared on "recommended" lists by various educational organizations—and still do. What I found was even more surprising. A significant number of these books had issues. Big issues. These recommended lists seemed to be based solely on availability rather than quality. Quality matters.

Common Issues With Decodable Texts

Below are the seven biggest and most common issues I found in currently available decodable texts. It is important that teachers avoid using texts with these issues.

1 Using low-utility words to try to squeeze in more words with the target skill

(e.g., *I can lug the cat with the rug. Let Lin dab a lip. Put it in the vat.*)

This issue has resulted from state decodability requirements and publisher competition. Some publishers began touting their decodable texts as better because they had a higher percentage of words that were decodable and more words with the target phonics skill in each book. On the surface, this made sense. But in application, it resulted in sentences like the examples above—sentences riddled with words not commonly used by children, thereby decreasing a child's comprehension of the text. The goal of early reading instruction is to match oral language with printed language. Thus, the sentences in these early readers are best when they more closely match children's speaking vocabularies.

2 Using non-standard English sentence structures

(e.g., *Ron did hit it. The pup did run at Kit.*)

Here again, this is the result of publishers trying to squeeze in more words with the target phonics skill without regard for comprehensibility. I have never uttered a sentence with "did hit" or "did run" in it, and I bet neither have most of you. All books for young readers should be models of good writing. Imagine how challenging these nonstandard sentences are for our English learners! All the sentences in decodable books must reflect common and natural-sounding English sentence patterns.

3 Using nonsensical sentences or tongue twisters

(e.g., *Slim Stan did spin, splat, stop. Fun Fran flips, flaps, flops. Mac had a bag. The bag had a dog. Mag had a rag. Mac can tag Mag.*)

The occasional use of alliteration can be fun in a decodable text. It can add an element of musicality that young readers enjoy. However, the consistent use of it throughout a book, as in the examples above, are quite detrimental to creating meaning from the text—the ultimate goal of reading it. The Mac/Mag example is even more commonplace, void of comprehensibility, and inexcusable.

4 Using too many easy referents or pronouns instead of specific concrete words, making the meaning difficult to figure out

(e.g., *She did not see it, but she did kick it.*)

Strong writing is clear writing. The reader understands easily who and what is being discussed. However, to create short and simple sentences, writers of decodable texts often overuse pronouns, such as *it, he,* and *she.* While the text "appears" easy to read, it is actually more difficult to understand because children have to make significantly more connections across sentences to get at meaning. In the example sentence, *"She did not see it,"* the reader must remember who "she" is from an earlier sentence and know what noun "it" refers to—either from an earlier sentence or the illustration. This increased propositional density of the text negatively affects comprehension. If the writer had written, *"Pam did not see the tiger,"* we would have readily understood the sentence's meaning without expending much cognitive energy. Since the word *tiger* is not decodable at this point in the year, the reader could have easily figured it out using the illustration. The word *tiger* would be an example of a story word, of which a couple in each book can add to the book's interest. Imagine the reader's delight at seeing a hidden tiger in the illustration and knowing that Pam, the main character, did not see it. How fast would that reader turn the page to see what happens next?

5 Using too simple language to explain scientific concepts due to phonics constraints

(e.g., *The sun will make plants rise.*)

This type of oversimplification of science concepts to create informational decodable texts can lead to misconceptions. I once worked on a series of early reading texts, which we sent to scientists at the prestigious Imperial College in London to review for accuracy. That is what all publishers need to do to maintain the highest standards with early learning tools.

6 Using odd names to get more decodable words in the story

(e.g., *Ben had Mem. Tam had the pup.*)

These uncommon, and sometimes made-up, names read as nonsense words to children. If there are too many of them in a story, it can make it difficult to remember the story's details, which will negatively affect comprehension. They can also be highly distracting to young readers.

7 Avoiding using the word *the* (the most common word in English)

This is the most confounding issue in decodable texts and is a direct result of state decodability requirements. The word *the* is the most common word in the English language. As a result, you would expect it to be all over early reading texts. Not so. Why? The word *the* is irregular, based on the common phonics skills taught to children; that is, it cannot be sounded out using those skills. So, every time a publisher includes *the*—the most common word in English—in a story, it decreases the story's decodability percentage. Since state decodability standards require a certain percentage of decodability, publishers remove the word *the* to meet those requirements. The result: stilted sentences that don't sound like English. Some states allow the word *the* to be counted as decodable when Long *e* spelled *e* (as in *he, me, we, she*) is taught. This is generally in mid-Grade 1 on most phonics scopes and sequences. So, for the first year and a half of reading instruction using decodable texts, the most common word in English is used sparingly and strategically, rather than naturally. It would be better if state reading requirements allowed the word *the* to count as decodable from the beginning of phonics instruction, the same way they do with the words *I* and *a*.

You might wonder how we arrived at an instructional tool so necessary, yet so poorly written. Much of it began with state reading adoption requirements specifying a decodable percentage that these books had to meet. When states began establishing these requirements, the California Department of Education required that decodable text be 75 percent controlled for phonics. Texas required 80 percent control. If publishers don't meet these requirements, they can't sell their books in those states. Since publishers can afford to create only one set of decodable texts, the higher 80-percent requirement has become the standard. As a result, writing these books has become more of a mathematical formula—trying to force a story into these strict requirements—than writing comprehensible and engaging texts that serve as a vital phonics practice tool.

There is *no* research that specifies that a decodable text must have a certain percentage of decodability. None. What researchers recommend is that the majority of the words can be sounded out based on the phonics skills children have learned. Irregular high-frequency words (e.g., *was, they*) and the occasional story words (e.g., *elephant*) create wonderful early reading experiences that are beneficial to the overall quality and comprehensibility of the text. Comprehensible. Instructive. Engaging. That should be the standard—not an arbitrary number.

I prefer to think about the texts we need for our youngest readers as *accountable texts*. We need texts wherein we can hold children accountable for the skills we have taught them (emphasizing phonics in the earliest years) and that provide us with a tool to evaluate their mastery of these skills. It's in the reading and writing of phonics skills where the learning sticks and in the authentic reading and writing where we can get our best formative assessment information to confirm the effectiveness of our instruction (or adjust that instruction as needed). That means that yes, it is beneficial if the majority of the words can be sounded out in the text using children's growing knowledge of phonics. But if one story is more comprehensible and engaging at 65 percent or 70 percent decodable than another story at 80 percent decodable that has stilted sentences and odd language structures, I prefer the story with the slightly lower decodability. Children will *still* get loads of decoding practice.

What Can I Do If My Decodable Texts Are Weak?

While finding stronger decodable texts is always the answer, that might not be feasible in the present or near future. I've worked with teachers to rewrite weaker decodable texts—both individual pages and entire books—and pasted over the existing text with the revision. The alternative is to create what I call *accountable sentences* to read after each lesson. This can consist of a numbered list of sentences (e.g., five for Kindergarten, ten for Grade 1). Each sentence contains at least one word with the target phonics skill. The other words are primarily decodable words or taught high-frequency words. The sentences can be on a topic you are reading about or discussing that week to give them more relevance, although that isn't necessary. It is much easier to create these accountable sentences than to write decodable stories.

Read these to your partner. Sign at the bottom of the page.

1. I see a frog.

2. I see a big frog.

3. The frog can hop.

4. The frog can hop in the pond.

5. Why? The frog is hot!

_____

The following pages show some examples of strong decodable texts.

Hen Pen's Joke

a retelling by Gail Tuchman

Hen Pen was sniffing a rose when something hit her hat.
"My, my!" she said. "The sky is falling. I must tell Wise King."

2

She hiked down the path and came upon Duck Luck.
"Wake up!" Hen Pen said.
With a poke, Duck Luck woke up.

3

The Frog Trail

by Judy Nayer

Sam waited and waited. In five weeks the tadpoles had legs.
"When will they be frogs?" Sam asked.

12

"Wait and see," said his father.
The next time Sam and his father went back to the lake, they saw lots of little frogs!

13

Name_____

I am Sam.

I can play soccer.

I like my dog, Rags.

Rags likes to play, too.

1

Name_____

This has six legs.

It is little.

It can hop.

What is it?   (grasshopper)

1

Newmark Learning (Benchmark Education) *Decodable Readers*

Short o

A Frog Can Jump

by Tammy Swann

It has no tail.

It is a frog!

A frog can jump up on a rock.

It can get a fat bug. *Snap!*

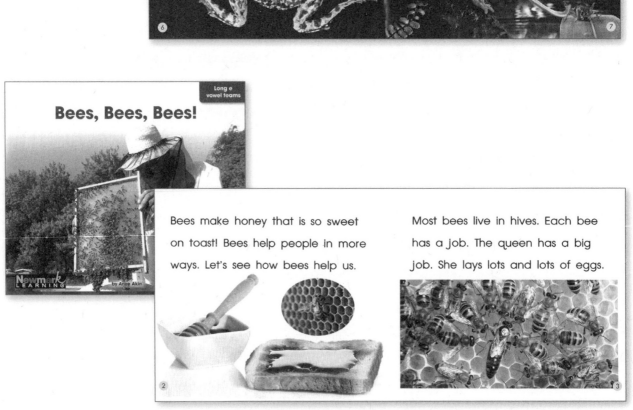

Long e vowel teams

Bees, Bees, Bees!

by Anne Akin

Bees make honey that is so sweet on toast! Bees help people in more ways. Let's see how bees help us.

Most bees live in hives. Each bee has a job. The queen has a big job. She lays lots and lots of eggs.

WHAT ROUTINES DO I USE WHEN TEACHING A DECODABLE TEXT TO BUILD PHONICS AND FLUENCY SKILLS?

We've discussed what decodable texts are and how to distinguish the highest-quality books and stories from those available. So, how do we teach using this essential phonics learning tool? In this chapter, we will examine high-impact activities to use *before, during*, and *after* reading decodable texts.

Before Reading

To prepare children for reading a decodable text, you must introduce the new target phonics skill practiced in the book and any new high-frequency words included. While variations exist in how reading materials do this, below is an example I use.

INTRODUCE THE NEW PHONICS SKILLS

Explicitly introduce the new sound (Long *a*) and target spelling (*a_e*).

For example: *The Long-a sound /ā/ can be spelled many ways. Today we will learn /ā/ spelled a_e, as in the word* m**a**k**e**.

Write the following on the board: **hat**
hate

Say: *Listen as I read each word:* hat, hate. *What sound is different?* (Hat *has the Short-a sound /a/;* hate *has the Long-a sound /ā/). Look at each word. What do you notice that is different?* (Hate *has an e at the end.) The letters* a *and* e *in the word* hate *work as a team so that the vowel* a *says its name: /ā/. Let's read some words with these Short- and Long-a sounds and spellings.*

MODEL BLENDING WORDS

Write a list of words (which I call *blending lines*) on the board for children to practice reading. You will guide them through the list. Model blending the first two words, then have children chorally read the rest. Tap on the word and prompt children to whisper-sound it out. Then tap again and have children chorally and loudly sound it out. Provide corrective feedback as needed. For children needing additional support, run your finger under the letters as they say and sing together each sound instead of the initial whisper-read. Then repeat, but faster.

Below is a sample blending-lines activity that I have differentiated. The lines go from easier to more complex to provide valuable formative assessment information. I also added review words to extend the learning of previously taught skills—which is necessary for many children to reach mastery so they can then transfer the skill. I also added a challenge line for students who are above level so that this activity has value for them as well.

Note: I use minimal contrasts in the first line—previously taught skill compared to the new skill—to go from the "known to the new" and emphasize the target skill. This makes the new learning more obvious for the student.

LINE 1 (minimal contrasts—new to known)	*hat hate tap tape bit bite*
LINE 2 (vary initial sound)	*bake take cake hide side slide*
LINE 3 (vary final sound)	*cake came made make bite bike*
LINE 4 (mixed set, target skill)	*game race page time smile price*
LINE 5 (review words for mastery)	*sing catch bank when which lunch*
LINE 6 (review words for mastery)	*spring flip stop brick grass clap*
LINE 7 (challenge words)	*tapping taping backing baking shaking liking*
LINE 8 (connected text)	*Jane came over to skate with us.*
LINE 9 (connected text)	*Mike likes to ride his bike.*

INTRODUCE THE NEW HIGH-FREQUENCY WORDS: READ/SPELL/WRITE/EXTEND

To introduce the new high-frequency words, I use the research-based Read/Spell/Write/Extend routine. Here is an example for the word *said*.

Step 1: Introduce in Context

Write a context sentence using the word. Underline the word. Read aloud the sentence, stressing the target word.

"I see a cat," <u>said</u> Pam.

Step 2: Read

Point to the word, read it aloud, and have children repeat. Then have them orally segment the word. Say: *What sounds do you hear in* said? *Let's tap them out: /s/ /e/ /d/. That's right. There are three sounds.* Next, highlight the parts of the word that are known and unknown. Say: *What is the first sound in* said? *(/s/) What letter do we write for the /s/ sound? (s) Do you see the letter s at the beginning of* said? *(Yes) What is the last sound in* said? *(/d/) What letter do we write for the /d/ sound? (d) Do you see the letter d at the end of* said? *(Yes) What is left? (ai) This is the part of* said *that does not follow the rules. This is the part we need to remember when reading and writing the word* said.

/s/ = s   /d/ = d   ai = irregular

Step 3: Spell

Have children chorally spell the word.

s-a-i-d

Step 4: Write

Have children write the word as they say each letter name. Prompt then to underline or circle the irregular part (*ai*).

s<u>ai</u>d

Step 5: Extend (Connect to Known Words/Writing)

Have children use the word in sentences. Provide oral and/or written sentence frames or sentence starters, as needed.

"I am _____," said the girl.

During Reading

Now it's time to read the decodable text. Children are ready after their introduction to the new phonics skill and the guided practice you provided reading words in isolation during the blending exercise. The primary task for you, the teacher, is to choose the best text possible. Make sure to select a text that meets the highest quality level—a text that is well-written and well-designed and meets the research criteria: **comprehensible** (follows natural-sounding English sentence structures and makes sense), **instructive** (ample words with the target phonics skill), and **engaging** (worth reading, talking about, writing about, and rereading to develop fluency). Be sure to include a good mix of fiction and informational decodable texts throughout your instruction. Strong decodable texts are available from Scholastic, Newmark Learning (Benchmark Education), and Sadlier.

READING A DECODABLE BOOK ROUTINE

Here is a general routine for reading a decodable text. On pages 80–85, I provide sample lessons for specific decodable texts to serve as models for the instruction you will deliver your students. I also provide a lesson planner on page 79.

Step 1: Preview and Predict

Read the title. Have children repeat. Describe the cover illustration (or photo) using key words to frontload vocabulary. Ask children to tell what they think the story will be about and why (noting details in the art and title). Preteach a new vocabulary word (Tier 2, academic word) that can be used to discuss the story but isn't in the story. (See the later discussion on this, page 75.)

Step 2: First Read (Read Together)

Have children point to each word as they chorally read it aloud. (You might wish to have children whisper-read it first as you circulate and listen in and offer support, or echo-read the story as you model an aspect of fluency.) If children have difficulty with any word, stop and provide corrective feedback. Then have them reread the sentence with the corrected word.

Sample Corrective Feedback: When children misread a word:

1. Point to the missed sound-spelling (e.g., *e*).

2. State the spelling and sound (e.g., *e* stands for the /e/ sound).

3. Have children repeat (e.g., *e, /e/*).

4. Ask children to blend the word again using the correction (e.g., /best/).

5. Have children go back to the start of the sentence and read it using the corrected word (e.g., *It is the best book!*).

Step 3: Check Comprehension

Ask questions about the story. Allow children to discuss answers with a partner before you call on a volunteer to answer. Prompt children to answer in complete sentences and find details in the text or art to support their answers.

Step 4: Second Read (Develop Fluency)

Have children reread the book to a partner. Circulate, listen in, and provide corrective feedback.

Step 5: Retell and Write

Have children retell the story to a partner in their own words. They can use the illustrations as cues to their retellings. Then have them write about the story. They can write their retelling, a story extension, a new story with the same characters, or what they learned from the book (if nonfiction). For extra support, use sentence starters and allow drawings.

Differentiating the Routine

Above-Level Students: I prefer having my above-level students read the decodable text the first day I introduce it so I can confirm they have mastered the phonics skill and can readily transfer it. However, on subsequent days when I have the other children reread the text to develop fluency or to prepare for writing about the text, I do not have my above-level students do this. It is a waste of their time. Instead, I pull them quickly to the front of the room (or at the small-group table) and work on a skill further in the phonics scope and sequence that they would benefit from. You can include the week's decodable texts in the children's book bags for independent or at-home reading, if appropriate.

Below-Level Students: Since my below-level students are still working on mastery of previously taught skills, this on-level text will be challenging. However, I know they will benefit from exposure to the text and the grade-level phonics skill focused on that week. To minimize their frustration, I have them listen to a recording of the text as they follow along prior to the whole-class lesson. Most publishers now offer digital recordings of their decodable texts. If none is available, I make my own recording. I have the students listen to the text and follow along a couple times. In addition, you can meet with these children during small-group time and guide them through a reading of the text to familiarize themselves with it. I generally do an echo-read, in which I read a sentence or page at a time (depending on length), and have children echo my reading. They can then listen to a digital recording of the book as follow-up and in preparation for the whole-group lesson.

After Reading

After reading a decodable text, it is important to check children's understanding of the text to reinforce the purpose of reading—to make meaning. In addition, a follow-up writing activity can deepen their comprehension and provide a targeted, scaffolded opportunity for children to write words using the new phonics skill introduced. I discuss in-depth how to check comprehension and extend the reading through writing in the chapters that follow. In addition to these essential after-reading activities, choose from the following activities to engage children in meaningful practice and conversations about how English words work.

- Write to Deepen Understanding (see Chapter 5, page 61)
- Check Comprehension (see Chapter 6, page 71)
- Word-Building
- Word Ladders
- Dictation
- High-Frequency Words (Read, Build, Write)
- Word Sorts
- Fluency Building

WORD-BUILDING

In word-building, you give children a set of letter cards and ask them to create a series of words in a specified sequence. Generally, each new word varies by only one sound-spelling from the previous word (there can be more variance as children progress in skills). For example, you might ask children to build, or make with letter cards, these words in sequence: *sat, mat, map, mop*. Notice how each word varies from the preceding word by only one sound-spelling. Select words from the decodable text and others to complete the activity.

Step 1: Introduce

Name the task and explain its purpose to children. Say: *Today we will be building, or making, words using the letters and spellings we have learned.*

Step 2: Model

Place letter cards in a pocket chart (or use letter cards on a whiteboard) to form the first word you are building. (Note: All children have the same letter-card set at their desks.) Model sounding out the word. Remember to:

- build words using the new, target sound-spelling
- add words with review sound-spellings as appropriate to extend the review and application of these skills to achieve mastery
- use minimal contrasts to require children to fully analyze words and notice their unique differences (e.g., *sat* and *mat, pan* and *pen, rip* and *trip, hat* and *hate, cot* and *coat*).

Say: *Look at the word I've made. It is spelled* s–a–t. *Let's blend the sounds together to read the word: /sssaaat/,* sat. *The word is* sat.

Step 3: Guided Practice/Practice

Continue by changing one (or more) letters in the word. Have children chorally blend the new word formed. Do a set of eight to ten words.

Say: *Change the letter* s *in* sat *to* m. *What is the new word?* Or, if children are more advanced in their understanding, say: *Change the first sound in* sat *to /m/.*

If the focus on word-building is word awareness (instead of blending, like the above example), then tell children what the next word in the sequence is and give them time to form the new word (e.g., change *sat* to *mat*). Circulate and provide assistance and corrective feedback (modeling your thinking process, modeling how to blend the word, and so on). Then build the new word in the pocket chart (or on the whiteboard), modeling aloud your thinking. I recommend word-building the first day by telling children what to change (e.g., change the letter *s* in *sat* to *m*), then on a subsequent day repeat the word-building by telling them what the next word should be (e.g. change *sat* to *mat*).

Sample Word-Building Word Sets

SET 1 (one skill): *sad, mad, map, tap, cap, cat*

SET 2 (multiple skills folded in): *sad, mad, map, mop, top, tap, cap, cat, cot*

WORD LADDERS

What distinguishes word ladders from the typical word-building exercise is the added element of vocabulary. Instead of asking children to build a word like *top,* then change it to make the word *mop,* you ask them to "change one letter in the word *top* to name something you use to clean a wet floor." Popularized by Timothy Rasinski, Ph.D. (2005), this is a fun activity to do at the end of the week when children have had multiple exposures to the words and know their meanings. Children love figuring out the clues, then determining how to make the new word. Select words from the week's decodable texts to complete the activity. Have children substitute, delete, or add a letter-sound to each word.

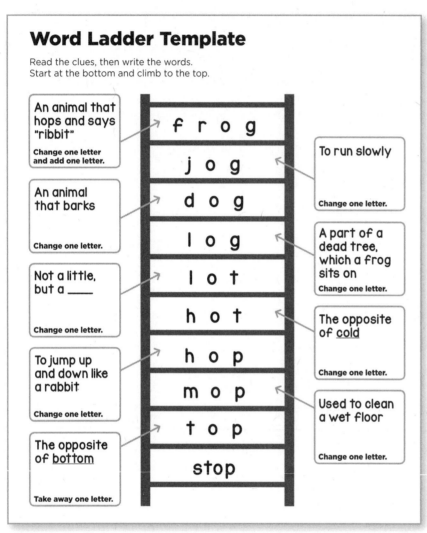

Word Ladder Template

Read the clues, then write the words.
Start at the bottom and climb to the top.

An animal that hops and says "ribbit"
Change one letter and add one letter.

f r o g

To run slowly
Change one letter.

j o g

An animal that barks
Change one letter.

d o g

A part of a dead tree, which a frog sits on
Change one letter.

l o g

Not a little, but a ____
Change one letter.

l o t

h o t

The opposite of <u>cold</u>
Change one letter.

To jump up and down like a rabbit
Change one letter.

h o p

m o p

Used to clean a wet floor
Change one letter.

The opposite of <u>bottom</u>
Take away one letter.

t o p

stop

(Rasinski, 2005)

DICTATION

Dictation is guided spelling practice. It is a way of modeling and providing supported practice in how to transfer phonics skills from reading to writing. In the primary grades, children's spelling ability generally lags behind their reading ability. That is, children can read words by applying specific phonics skills before they can consistently write words accessing those same skills. Thus, they need lots of guided practice using their phonics skills in writing. Choose a few words from the decodable text for children to spell after the reading. Model by thinking aloud how to spell these words.

Step 1: State the Word and Provide Supports

State aloud the first word in the dictation exercise, and have children repeat it. For those who have difficulty hearing the sounds in the words, you can provide two levels of support. One level involves saying the sounds more slowly and moving your hands from right to left while facing the class to illustrate beginning, middle, and end. A second level of assistance involves modeling the segmenting of the sounds in the word (e.g., by tapping, using sound boxes, page 66). In effect, this helps children hear and write one sound at a time.

Step 2: Have Children Write

Next, have children write the word. Walk around the room and give help as necessary. This may include showing them the correct stroke procedure for writing letters or directing them to the correct spelling on the alphabet wall chart or frieze. In the case of multiple spellings for a single sound (such as *c, k,* and *ck*), tell children which spelling is correct and briefly explain why. For example, the *ck* spelling for /k/ appears at the end of a word and is preceded by a short-vowel sound (e.g., *sick, back, rock, luck, deck*). Continue this procedure for each word in the dictation line. For the dictation sentence, read the entire sentence aloud and then focus on one word at a time. For multisyllabic words, do one syllable at a time.

Step 3: Offer Feedback

As children complete each word, provide feedback by writing the answer on the board so that they can correct their work. A key component of dictation is self-correction, in which children begin to notice and correct their errors.

Sample Dictation Word Sets

(Words with new skill)	*up, mud, run*
(Words with review skills)	*bed, zip*
(Simple sentence)	*We had a lot of fun!*

HIGH-FREQUENCY WORDS

Select the target high-frequency words from the decodable text and any others that children struggle with and engage them in this Read, Build, Write activity.

- **Read** Write the word. Have children read it aloud.
- **Build** Have children build the word using letter cards.
- **Write** Have children write the word on paper or a dry-erase board. Prompt them to say each letter name as they write the word.

When completed, guide children to orally segment the sounds in the word. Then review the written parts of the word children already know (e.g., for the word *said,* children might know the /s/ sound spelled *s* and the /d/ sound spelled *d*). Guide them to draw a circle or box around the part(s) of the word that is irregular (e.g., *ai* in the word *said*) or unknown based on the phonics skills previously taught.

Children can write sentences during independent-work time for each of these words. To scaffold the exercise, offer sentence starters (e.g., *We have* _____). Prompt children to write sentences about a specific topic or story they recently read to make the exercise more impactful.

WORD SORTS

Word sorts also allow children time to think about how words work by drawing their attention to important and common spelling patterns. Generally, in word sorts, you give children a set of words that have something in common (e.g., all contain the same vowel sound, but with different spellings, as in *-at* and *-an* words for Short *a*). You then ask children to sort the words by their common feature. Select words from two or three word families from the decodable text. You will probably need to add words to have at least four or five for each word family in the sort.

Step 1: Introduce

Name the task and explain its purpose. Distribute the word cards and read each with children to make sure they know all the words. If you are doing a closed sort, introduce the categories in which children will be sorting the words.

Step 2: Sort

Invite children to sort the words. If you are doing a closed sort, model sorting one or two of the words. Then have children sort the remaining words. Circulate and ask them questions about why they are putting specific words into each category.

Step 3: Check and Discuss

Review the words in each sort category. Ask children what they learned about these words from doing the sort. Guide them to the word-awareness aspect of each sort that will assist them in reading and writing. This discussion about what children observe about words from doing the sort is the *real value* in the activity. Have them store the word cards for future sorts (e.g., a timed sort using these words).

Sample Word Sort Word Sets	
Short *a*:	*__at, __an, mat, sat, cat, man, can, ran*
Short *u*:	*__ug, __un, bug, rug, dug, fun, sun, run*

FLUENCY BUILDING

Repeated readings is one of the most research-proven ways to build a child's fluency. Create a repeated-reading routine for children to follow during independent-work time. You can also incorporate this routine into your small-group work. For example, each lesson can begin with a quick repeated reading of a previously read book or story while you circulate and listen in. Use key decodable readers and other weekly texts for these rereadings. Below is a sample routine.

Repeated-Reading Fluency Routine

Day 1: Reread the decodable book/story from the previous week independently and/or to a partner.

Day 2: Reread the decodable book/story from two weeks ago. Locate and record words with a specific phonics skill (provided by the teacher).

Day 3: Reread the decodable book/story from three weeks ago. Write a summary of the story.

Day 4: Reread the decodable book/story from this week to a partner.

Day 5: Select a previously read decodable book/story to read to a partner while the teacher conducts fluency checks (listens to children read aloud). Children take home a decodable book/story from this week to read to families.

Use the forms and templates on the following pages to assist you in these After-Reading activities.

- Fluency Activity Checklist (page 48)
- Word-Sort Template (page 50)
- Word-Building Template (page 52)
- Word Ladder Template (page 54)
- Read, Build, Write Template (page 55)
- Blending Line Templates for Grades K–2 (page 57)

Fluency Activity Checklist

Below are some additional routines and activities that will be helpful in building children's fluency using the decodable readers and other classroom books. Also, continue to model fluent reading as you read aloud, pointing out specific aspects of fluency.

- Focus on intonation and phrasing.
- Teach children how to use end marks to change how they read a sentence and remind them to read dialogue the way the character would have said the words.
- Pull out sentences from weekly readings, model one aspect of fluent reading (e.g., intonation using end marks, phrasing based on prepositions), and have children repeat/mimic your model. Continue to reinforce that skill throughout the week's readings.

ROUTINE AND ACTIVITY	WHAT TO DO
☐ Echo Read	Introduce the echo-reading procedure you will use to model fluency and practice repeated readings. Use one of the week's stories to model. In echo reading, you read a phrase or sentence in the text, then children repeat it, mimicking your rate and intonation. Use this technique to introduce children to a new text in future lessons.
☐ Choral Read	Introduce the choral-reading procedures you will use to model fluency and practice repeated readings. Use one of the week's stories to model. In choral reading, you guide children in an "out-loud" oral reading of a text as a group. Remind them to "keep their voices with yours" as you read with them. Use this technique to engage children in repeated readings of future connected text passages.
☐ Oral Recitation Lesson	This fluency technique focuses on comprehension. Introduce one of the stories you are reading with children this week. Read it aloud. Discuss it and co-create a story summary with children. Then select one prosodic element to model in the text, such as using end punctuation to vary voice. Then have children practice reading sections of the text both on their own and with your support. Finally, have them read sections of the text aloud for the class. Monitor each child's reading rate and word accuracy.

ROUTINE AND ACTIVITY	WHAT TO DO
☐ Reader's Theater	One of the most engaging ways to build fluency is through the use of Reader's Theater passages. Children select parts to practice and read aloud for the class. If no Reader's Theater passages are available, choose a selection from the week that contains a lot of dialogue or is easily divided into individual parts.
☐ Audiobook Modeling	Throughout the year, provide children with audio recordings of books to listen to fluent models. Explain to children that they will listen to how a good reader reads aloud and can use this model to improve their own fluency. Select an audiobook at or a bit above children's reading level. Have children listen to the audio recording as they follow along in the print book. Tell them to stop at the end of each page or spread and reread using the same pace, phrasing, and expression. They can listen to the page as many times as needed to practice. Finally, have children read the book and record their reading.
☐ Oral Reading Modeling	Explain to children that in order to be fluent readers, they need to pay attention to and practice the traits of skilled readers. These include reading at the correct speed, reading the words in a text with ease, and raising and lowering their voice appropriately when reading. Select a short story or passage from the week. Read it aloud expressively. Discuss the passage. Create a one- to three-sentence summary. Discuss elements of the text, such as reading dialogue as if it is spoken and the difference between statements, exclamations, and questions. Then prompt children to practice reading the selection with partners and independently. Select children to listen to and record notes regarding their intonation, rate, and accuracy.
☐ Repeated Readings Chart	Having children occasionally chart their own reading progress can be highly motivating. Have children read one of the week's stories for one minute. Have them mark where they stopped when the time ran out. Ask them to count the number of words read. If available, guide them to chart the number on a graph. Then, have children independently practice reading the passage over the next couple days. At the end of the week, have them reread the passage for one minute and mark where they stopped. Prompt them to compare how much further they were able to read.

Word-Sort Template

Teacher: Write the word-sort words and categories in the boxes. See the example on the following page.

Word-Sort Sample: Short *a*

__at	__an	cat
mat	sat	bat
hat	fan	can
pan	ran	man

Word-Building Template

Teacher: Write the word-building letters in the boxes. Use no more than 10 letters. See the example on the following page.

Word-Building Sample: Short *a* and *o*

a	o	s
t	m	p
n		

Words: sat, mat, map, mop, top, tap, pat, pan, man

Word Ladder Template

Read the clues, then write the words.
Start at the bottom and climb to the top.

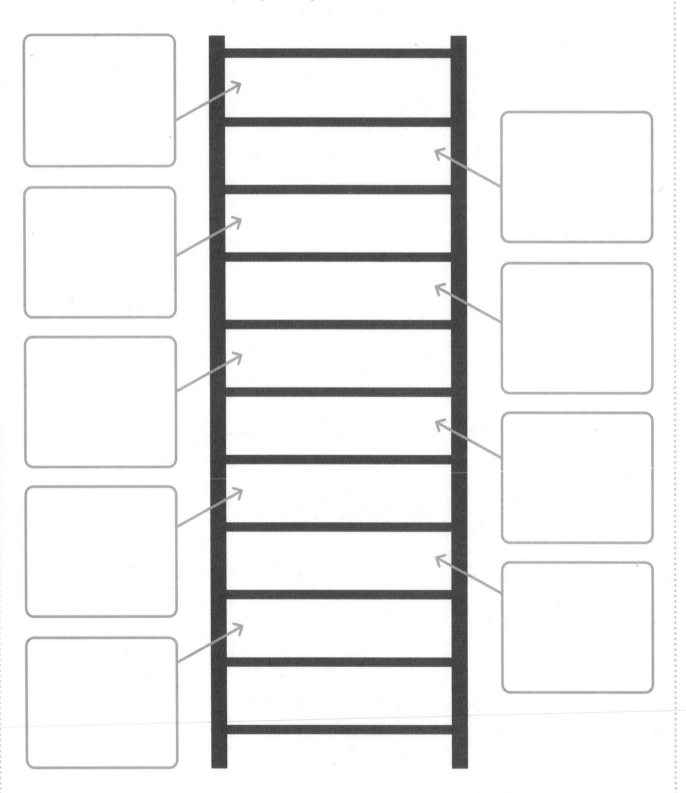

Read, Build, Write Template

Read each word. Build it with letter cards. Then write the word.

Read	Build	Write

Teacher: Write high-frequency words in the first column. See the example on the following page.

Read, Build, Write Sample

Read each word. Build it with letter cards. Then write the word.

Read	Build	Write
the		
is		
like		
see		

t	h	e	i	s	l	k	e

Blending Line Templates for Grades K–2

KINDERGARTEN

Line 1 (letter-sounds)	
Line 2 (new skill, minimal contrasts)	
Line 3 (new skill)	
Line 4 (review words)	
Line 5 (challenge words)	
Line 6 (connected text)	
Line 7 (connected text)	

GRADE 1

Line 1 (minimal contrasts—new to known)	
Line 2 (vary initial sound)	
Line 3 (vary final sound)	
Line 4 (mixed set, target skill)	
Line 5 (review words for mastery)	
Line 6 (review words for mastery)	
Line 7 (challenge words)	
Line 8 (connected text)	
Line 9 (connected text)	

Blending Line Templates (continued)

Check Foundational Skills

Line 1	
Line 2	
Line 3	

Transition to Longer Words

Line 4	
Line 5	

Challenge

Line 6	
Line 7	

Reading in Context

Line 8	
Line 9	

Choosing and Using Decodable Texts © 2021 by Wiley Blevins, Scholastic Inc. • page 58

Blending Line Samples for Grades K–2

KINDERGARTEN

Line 1 (letter-sounds)	h i a d
Line 2 (new skill, minimal contrasts)	hat sat mat cat
Line 3 (new skill)	has hat his hit
Line 4 (review words)	did mad fan can
Line 5 (challenge words)	hats hits fans maps
Line 6 (connected text)	Dad has a hat.
Line 7 (connected text)	I hid it!

GRADE 1

Line 1 (minimal contrasts— new to known)	hat hate tap tape bit bite
Line 2 (vary initial sound)	bake take cake hide side slide
Line 3 (vary final sound)	cake came made make bite bike
Line 4 (mixed set, target skill)	game race page time smile price
Line 5 (review words for mastery)	sing catch bank when which lunch
Line 6 (review words for mastery)	spring flip stop brick grass clap
Line 7 (challenge words)	tapping taping backing baking shaking liking
Line 8 (connected text)	Jane came over to skate with us.
Line 9 (connected text)	Mike likes to ride his bike.

Blending Line Samples (continued)

Check Foundational Skills

Line 1	lap clap back black lip flip
Line 2	rip drip cab crab tuck truck
Line 3	top stop sell smell sack snack

Transition to Longer Words

Line 4	spell spelling stack stacking cross crossing
Line 5	spot spotless frost frostbite drop droplets

Challenge

Line 6	classroom slippery springtime flashlight streetcar grasshopper
Line 7	playground blizzard president dragonfly crossword breakfast

Reading in Context

Line 8	Brad put a green and red flag on his truck.
Line 9	Stan got to swim on his trip to Florida.

HOW DO I CONNECT DECODABLE TEXTS TO WRITING?

One of the most underused activities during phonics instruction is writing. When writing, children must bring together all they know about how words work and combine that with their comprehension of the text to express their understandings. It is not only an extremely effective phonics practice/application activity; it is a great informal assessment of student progress.

Since writing words with new phonics skills generally lags behind a child's ability to read words with those skills, writing gives us powerful insights into a child's level of phonics mastery over time. By monitoring children's consistent use of specific phonics skills in their writing (or noticing early on when they cannot apply previously taught skills), we can modify our teaching to better meet their instructional needs.

When children read a **fiction** decodable text, have them do one of the following as a writing follow-up:

- Write a retelling
- Write a story extension (What happens next?)
- Put the characters in a new setting
- Insert yourself into the story and rewrite it

When children read an **informational** decodable text, have them do one of the following as a writing follow-up:

- Make a list of three facts learned
- Draw a picture based on the selection and write one to three sentences to describe it, using details from the selection and drawing
- Write about the most interesting or surprising thing you learned
- Summarize what you learned and write what else you would like to know about the topic (in a series of questions)

When children need support spelling a word, guide them to orally segment the word then attach a spelling to each sound. Model as needed. This modeling should begin in formal dictation exercises (see template below) in which you select three or four words with the new phonics skill for children to spell, then guide them through the process—thinking aloud about how you spell the word (e.g., *I hear the /s/ sound as the beginning of* sat, *so I will write the letter* s. *The next sound I hear is . . .*).

Keep a list of previously taught phonics skills on a note card. When reviewing a child's writing, take note of skills he or she is not consistently and accurately using. You might wish to staple a copy of the year's phonics scope and sequence into each student's writing notebook. (See Transfer Chart sample on the following page.) Circle each skill on the list as you introduce it. Put a check beside the skill when you notice the child's successful, consistent use of the skill in writing. Periodically review these charts for all your students and adjust instruction accordingly. For example, you might need to do more dictation exercises for skills many children struggle with. Or, you can form small groups based on skills a handful of children need additional instruction and practice on.

Grade 1 Phonics: Transfer Chart for Writing Notebook

Skill	Mastery	Examples	Skill	Mastery	Examples
Short *a*	✓	man sad hat	Digraph *sh*, Digraph *th* (both sounds)		
Short *i*	✓	it sit did	Digraph *ch*, *tch*, Digraph *wh*		
Short *o*	✓	on Mom hop	Digraph *ng* (also cover *nk*)		
Short *u*	✓	up fun sun	Final *e* (a_e, i_e)		
Short *e*	✓	red get tell	Final *e* (o_e, u_e, e_e)		
l-blends	✓	slip clap	Single-Letter Long Vowels *e, i, o*		
s-blends	✓	stop smell	Long *a* (*ai, ay*)		
r-blends					

Extra Supports

For children who need additional supports while writing, encourage them to use the decodable text as a reference. In addition, provide sound (Elkonin) boxes (page 66) and counters for children who need more guidance segmenting a word and associating each sound to a letter or spelling.

To use the sound boxes, make sure children can stretch a word. For example, tell children that you want to stretch the word *sat* like a rubber band. Say *ssssaaat* as you move your hands in a stretching motion. Then tell them that you want to mark each sound in the word. To do so, you will stretch the word again. Then drag one counter onto each box on the Elkonin box as you move from sound to sound. Ask children to repeat using their Elkonin boxes and counters.

Connecting Reading to Writing

Here's an example of a decodable text and the follow-up writing assignment. This is a Grade 1 text I wrote for children to begin applying the new phonics skill Long *a* (spelled *ai* and *ay*). By this point in the phonics scope and sequence, children have learned all their short vowels (*a, e, i, o, u*), final *e* (*a_e, i_e, e_e, o_e, u_e*), consonant blends (*l-, r-,* and *s*-blends), consonant digraphs (*wh, sh, ch, tch, th, ng*), and several important high-frequency words (e.g., *to, do, what, one, for, or, the, live*). Therefore, this text is highly accountable based on the skills children have been taught. The story contains only two story words (*museum, castle*) that are clearly shown in the illustrations.

My Big Trip

Last May, I went to Spain.
It was a fun trip.
What did I do there?
Take a look!

One day, I rode in a train.
I paid a lot for the ride.
I went to see a museum.
I had to wait in a long line
to get inside.

The next day, it rained.
I went to see a castle.
A castle is a big home
for a king or queen.
But the King of Spain
doesn't live in this one.

Spain is a fun place to visit.
When I go away next spring,
maybe I will go back.
But I hope it doesn't rain again!

WRITING FOLLOW-UP

Since stories such as this contain many words with the new phonics skills, writing about them is an essential and highly beneficial follow-up activity because it requires children to use (spell) words with the new skill.

> Write a retelling of the story. Include the places where the girl went, what she saw there, and what you learned about Spain. Use the words and pictures for ideas.
>
> ---
>
> Tyler
>
> The grl went to Spain. She saw a palis. A king livs there. It raind in Spain a lot!

Use the forms and templates on the following pages to assist you in the dictation activities.

- Sound (Elkonin) Boxes (page 66)
- Dictation Templates: Kindergarten and Grade 1 (pages 67 and 68)
- Grade 1 Phonics: Transfer Chart for Writing Notebook (page 69)

Sound (Elkonin) Boxes

Dictation Template: Kindergarten

Letter-Sounds

Listen to each picture name. Write the first letter of the picture name on the line.

1.

picture

2.

picture

Words: Guided Practice

Listen to each picture name. Write the letter for each sound in a separate box.

3.

picture

4.

picture

Words and Sentence: Independent

Write the word and sentence that you hear.

5.

6.

Dictation Template: Grade 1

Words: Guided Practice

Listen to each picture name. Write the letter for each sound in a separate box.

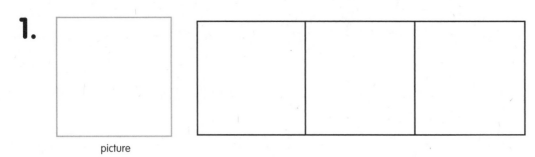

1. picture

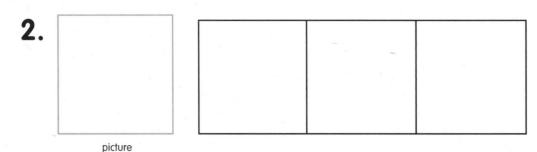

2. picture

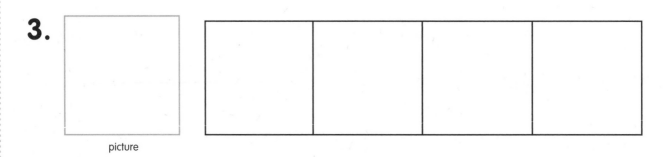

3. picture

Words and Sentence: Independent

Write each word and sentence that you hear.

4. _____   **5.** _____

6. _____

Grade 1 Phonics: Transfer Chart for Writing Notebook

Skill	Mastery	Examples
Short *a*		
Short *i*		
Short *o*		
Short *u*		
Short *e*		
l-blends		
s-blends		
r-blends		

Skill	Mastery	Examples
Digraph *sh*, Digraph *th* (both sounds)		
Digraph *ch, tch*, Digraph *wh*		
Digraph *ng* (also cover *nk*)		
Final *e* (a_e, i_e)		
Final *e* (o_e, u_e, e_e)		
Single-Letter Long Vowels e, i, o		
Long *a* (*ai, ay*)		

Grade 1 Phonics: Transfer Chart (continued)

Skill	Mastery	Examples
Long *e* (*ee, ea*)		
Long *o* (*oa, ow*)		
Long *i* (*y, igh*)		
Long *u* (*u, ew, ue*)		
r-Controlled *ar*		
r-Controlled *er, ir, ur*		
r-Controlled *or, ore, oar*		
Short *oo* [*book*], Long *oo* (*oo, ou, ew, ue, u_e*) [*room*]		

Skill	Mastery	Examples
Diphthong /ou/ (*ou, ow*)		
Diphthong /oi/ (*oi, oy*)		
Complex Vowel /â/ (*au, aw, a*[*lk*], *a*[*lt*], *a*[*ll*])		
r-Controlled *are, air, ear*		
Long *i* and *o* (*i*[*ld*], *i*[*nd*], *o*[*ld*])		
Long *i* and *o* (*ie, oe*)		
Long *e* (*y, ey, ie, ei*)		

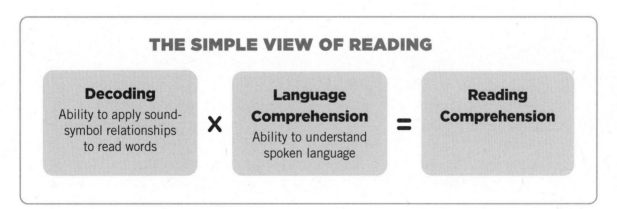

HOW DO I EXTEND THE USE OF DECODABLE TEXTS TO BUILD COMPREHENSION AND VOCABULARY?

The current national conversation around the Science of Reading clarifies the important role of phonics in early reading development. As we collect information from multiple disciplines—including educational researchers, cognitive scientists, speech pathologists, and so on—we are broadening and deepening our understanding of what comprises the most effective early reading instruction. Two older models of reading have been reintroduced to teachers to clarify that instruction: The Simple View of Reading by Gough and Tunmer (1986), and Scarborough's Reading Rope (2001).

The Simple View of Reading explains that reading comprehension is a product of decoding (all the work we do with phonics) and language comprehension (e.g., vocabulary and background knowledge). One without the other does <u>not</u> lead to skilled readers who can readily understand the texts they need to tackle at each grade level.

THE SIMPLE VIEW OF READING

Decoding
Ability to apply sound-symbol relationships to read words

X

Language Comprehension
Ability to understand spoken language

=

Reading Comprehension

(Gough & Tunmer, 1986; Hoover & Gough, 1990)

Scarborough's Reading Rope clarifies the Simple View of Reading and illustrates how as children become more fluent in their word-recognition skills (e.g., through phonics) and more strategic in using their language-comprehension skills, these skills begin to intertwine—creating skilled, fluent readers capable of comprehending more complex texts.

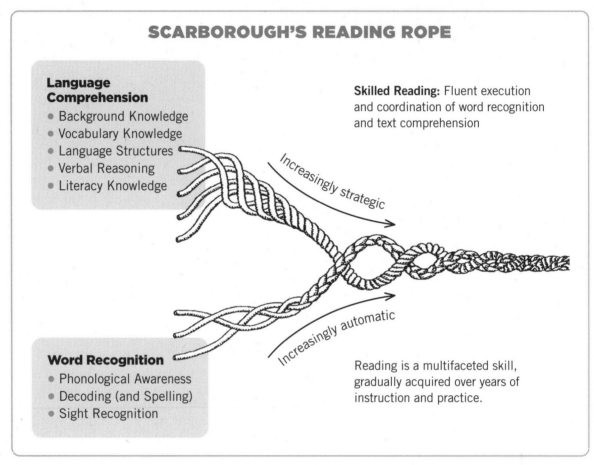

SCARBOROUGH'S READING ROPE

Language Comprehension
- Background Knowledge
- Vocabulary Knowledge
- Language Structures
- Verbal Reasoning
- Literacy Knowledge

Skilled Reading: Fluent execution and coordination of word recognition and text comprehension

Increasingly strategic

Increasingly automatic

Word Recognition
- Phonological Awareness
- Decoding (and Spelling)
- Sight Recognition

Reading is a multifaceted skill, gradually acquired over years of instruction and practice.

(Scarborough, 2001)

Both of these models of reading highlight the critical role phonics plays. They also emphasize that phonics alone is not enough. In addition, the phonics instruction we deliver must be aware of grade-level reading demands while simultaneously meeting children where they are (necessitating two-tier instruction—whole group for grade-level exposure of skills and small group to meet individual needs).

These models also reveal why we must include more robust comprehension and vocabulary work during our decodable text-reading lessons. There is so much more we can do to develop children's understanding of these simple texts while also building strong early reading behaviors. In addition, because most of the vocabulary words in decodable texts are common, Tier 1 words, we don't think of these texts as ripe for building vocabulary (unless the student is an English learner). However, there is much we can do on that front as well.

Extending Reading to Comprehension and Vocabulary

Here's the same decodable text from the previous chapter, followed by the comprehension questions asked about it, and how I help children develop vocabulary. This is a Grade 1 text I wrote for children to begin applying the new phonics skill Long *a* (spelled *ai* and *ay*).

My Big Trip

Last May, I went to Spain.
It was a fun trip.
What did I do there?
Take a look!

One day, I rode in a train.
I paid a lot for the ride.
I went to see a museum.
I had to wait in a long line
to get inside.

The next day, it rained.
I went to see a castle.
A castle is a big home
for a king or queen.
But the King of Spain
doesn't live in this one.

Spain is a fun place to visit.
When I go away next spring,
maybe I will go back.
But I hope it doesn't rain again!

COMPREHENSION QUESTIONS

Below are the questions I ask children after reading the text. The questions get progressively more complex. I have children discuss each answer with a partner *before* I call on volunteers to answer so all children are using language and processing their understanding of the text. Note that I require them to supply text evidence to support their answers—an important reading behavior to develop. (See Comprehension Questions Template, page 78.)

1. Where did the girl go? Point to the country's name in the story.	This question focuses children's attention on a word with the new phonics skill.
2. What did the girl do in Spain? Find the sentences that tell this.	This question directs children's attention to details in the text and requires them to provide text evidence to support their answer—an important skill for all readers.
3. What problems did the girl have? Circle them. Why were they problems?	This is a higher-order thinking question requiring children to pull together various pieces of information and directing them to find the details that will help them.
4. Where might the girl go next? Why do you think this?	This is a more complex question that requires children to draw some conclusions based on text evidence and their prior knowledge.
5. Where might you like to go on a big trip? Tell your partner why.	This question connects the story to children's lives.

BUILDING VOCABULARY

While teaching children how to decode words, we also need to spend equal amounts of time expanding their vocabularies and background knowledge. This is essential in order for children to comprehend more complex texts as they move up the grades. Typically, we focus on vocabulary and content-knowledge building during read-alouds and the interactive discussions we have about them. But we shouldn't lose a single opportunity to build children's listening and speaking vocabularies. And, we can do that with simple decodable texts. How?

- With each book, select a more-sophisticated academic word (not in the story) that you can use to talk <u>about</u> the story.
- Preteach that word when introducing the book or introduce it at the point of the story where it's most appropriate.
- Ask questions about the book using the word, and prompt children to use the word in their answers.

For example, if you are reading a story about a boy who gets a dog and gives the dog food, water, and a home, then the story is about survival. Introduce the word *survive* before reading the story using the Define-Example-Ask routine (below). Then ask questions while reading to guide children to use the word (e.g., *How is the boy helping the dog survive on this page?*).

Define: *Survive* means "to live."

Example: A dog needs food, water, and air to survive, or live.

Ask: What do you need to survive?

Here's another example, from when I was introducing a decodable story called *Lots of Frogs*. The cover showed an illustration of some frogs at a pond. The illustration was such a clear example of the frog's habitat, that I introduced the word *habitat* to children when I introduced the book by using the cover illustration. As we read, I directed children to look for details in the text and art (there were many details in the art) that told us more about a frog's habitat. I prompted them to use the word *habitat* in their discussion about the story.

> ## Building Vocabulary With "My Big Trip"
>
> Tell children: *Today we're going to read a story about a girl who travels to a new place and learn about all the things she explored.*
>
> **Define:** *Explore* means "to find out more about something."
>
> **Example:** In science today, we will explore the plants and animals living in the pond near our school.
>
> **Ask:** What new place would you like to explore, or find out more about?

Other Activities to Support Vocabulary Development

Read-Aloud: Connect your daily read-aloud to the decodable text. For example, if you are reading a simple decodable book about frogs, read an informational picture book about frogs, such as *Red-Eyed Tree Frog* by Joy Cowley. Highlight academic words, such as *habitat* and *life cycle,* during the conversation about the book. Then, when reading the decodable text, continue to use these academic words when talking about the illustrations, photos, and text in this simpler book. Use the academic words in your questions about the book, and prompt children to use these words when answering questions, discussing, or writing about the book. Making this tight connection between a decodable book and a daily read-aloud is certainly *not* always possible, but when the connection can be made it is powerful.

Wide Reading: Each week, provide additional books around the decodable book's topic to increase wide reading on that topic, including your daily read-alouds. This wide reading can reinforce critical vocabulary and deepen children's background knowledge.

English-Learner Supports

Even though the words in decodable texts are often basic, Tier 1 words, some words in these books might be unknown to multilingual learners who are learning English as an additional language and native English-speaking students with limited literacy backgrounds. For example, I've seen words such as *log, tad, sip, cap, vet, zap,* and others that might be unknown to some children. What can you do?

I recommend selecting a set of these words each week and teaching them during small-group time. The goal is for children to be able to both read and define them by the end of the week. To really know a word, we need to focus on its meaning, sounds and spelling, and the context in which it is used. For example, for the word *bat,* we would discuss the word's multiple meanings (a flying animal and something used in a baseball game to hit the ball). For the word *rain,* we might discuss what it is, what we wear on a rainy day, and what time of year it usually rains. So, during these targeted vocabulary lessons do the following:

- Read aloud the word in English and the child's primary language. You can use a translation app on your phone for children to hear the word in their primary language.

- Provide a brief definition. Demonstrate, act out, or pantomime the word.

- Connect the word to known words. Start with synonyms and antonyms. For example, for the word *cap,* connect it to the more familiar word *hat*. For the word *sad,* connect it to the opposite— *happy*.

- Display a photo or create a simple drawing to illustrate the word. For example, words like *bug, log,* and *hut* can be easily shown. However, illustrations are sometimes not available.

All of these activities can increase the impact decodable texts have on children's reading and writing development. On the following pages are a lesson template to plan your instruction and a comprehension-questions form to use during follow-up conversations.

Comprehension Questions Template

Book Title: _____

1.	This question focuses children's attention on a word with the new phonics skill.
2.	This question directs children's attention to text details and requires them to provide text evidence to support their answer.
3.	This is a higher-order thinking question.
4.	This is a higher-order thinking question.
5.	This question connects the story to children's lives.

Choosing and Using Decodable Texts © 2021 by Wiley Blevins, Scholastic Inc. • page 78

Decodable Text Lesson Planner

Book Title:

Focus Phonics Skill:

Decodable Words With Phonics Skill:

New High-Frequency and Story Words:

BEFORE READING

Academic Vocabulary Word About the Book:

- **Define:**

- **Example:**

- **Ask:**

English-Learner Supports (e.g., vocabulary to preteach):

DURING READING

Technique (choral read, echo read, whisper read):

AFTER READING

Comprehension Questions:

1. (focus on word with phonics skill)

2. (detail with text evidence)

3. (higher-level question)

4. (higher-level question)

5. (connect to children's lives)

Writing Prompt:

Fluency Plan:

SAMPLE DECODABLE TEXT LESSONS

Following are sample lessons to use with the reproducible decodable mini-books on pages 87–126.

Let's Grow Them (page 87)

Focus Phonics Skill: Short e

Decodable Words With Phonics Skill: *Jess, red, Ben, ten, get, wet*

New High-Frequency and Story Words: *are, grow, let's, yes, you*

BEFORE READING

Academic Vocabulary Word About the Book: *patient*

- **Define:** waiting quietly for something
- **Example:** The kids were patient as they waited for the recess bell to ring.
- **Ask:** When have you had to be patient?

English-Learner Supports (e.g., vocabulary to preteach): *seeds, grow, dig, red, can* (noun)

DURING READING

Technique (choral read, echo read, whisper read): Have children whisper-read the story while you listen in and offer feedback. Then, echo-read the story, modeling how the end mark affects how you read each sentence—period, question mark, exclamation point.

AFTER READING

Comprehension Questions:

1. **(focus on word with phonics skill)** How many seeds does Ben have? (*ten*) Find the word in the story.

2. **(detail with text evidence)** What did Ben and Jess do to help the seeds grow? Find the sentences that support your answer.

3. **(higher-level question)** Why did Ben and Jess have to wait so long?

4. **(higher-level question)** Do you think Ben and Jess were patient? Why or why not?

5. **(connect to children's lives)** Have you ever planted seeds or watched a plant grow? If so, what did you observe, or see?

Writing Prompt: Have children make a list of the steps to grow tomatoes.

Fluency Plan: Have children reread the story to a partner on the following day. On a later day, have them reread the story to find (circle or list) words with -*en* and -*et*.

No Fun for Gus! (page 95)

Focus Phonics Skill: Short *u*

Decodable Words With Phonics Skill: *mud, stuck, tub, bug, drum, gum, bun, fun, bus, Gus*

New High-Frequency and Story Words: *his, missed, then*

BEFORE READING

Academic Vocabulary Word About the Book: *enjoy*

- **Define:** to like or have fun

- **Example:** I enjoy reading and cooking.

- **Ask:** What do you enjoy doing?

English-Learner Supports (e.g., vocabulary to preteach): *bus, drum, bun, bug, stuck, cap, mud, tub*

DURING READING

Technique (choral read, echo read, whisper read): Echo-read the first reading, modeling how the end mark affects how you read each sentence—period, question mark, exclamation point. Then choral-read the second reading.

AFTER READING

Comprehension Questions:

1. **(focus on word with phonics skill)** What bit Gus's leg? (*bug*) Find the word in the story.

2. **(detail with text evidence)** Why did Gus have to get in the tub? Find the sentences that support your answer.

3. **(higher-level question)** What does Gus enjoy doing? Why do you think so?

4. **(higher-level question)** Do you think Gus is having a good day? Why or why not?

5. **(connect to children's lives)** What do you do for fun when you are having a bad day?

Writing Prompt: Have children write a retelling of the story.

Fluency Plan: Have children reread the story to a partner on the following day. On a later day, have them reread the story to find (circle or list) words with *-un* and *-um*. Have them write words that rhyme with *bug*.

The Three Little Pigs (page 103)

Focus Phonics Skill: Long *e* (*ea, ee*)

Decodable Words With Phonics Skill: *leaped, mean, please, read, feet, free, see, sleep, three, eat, heat*

New High-Frequency and Story Words: *away, I'll, one, over, toes*

BEFORE READING

Academic Vocabulary Word About the Book: *dilemma*

- **Define:** a problem in which you must make a difficult choice
- **Example:** The family had a big dilemma during the hurricane—stay home and risk getting trapped or leave quickly without everything they owned.
- **Ask:** What is a dilemma you have had to deal with?

English-Learner Supports (e.g., vocabulary to preteach): *leaped, mean, chimney, grass, sticks, logs, huff and puff*

DURING READING

Technique (choral read, echo read, whisper read): Have children whisper-read the story while you listen in and offer feedback. Then echo-read, modeling reading dialogue as the character would have said it.

AFTER READING

Comprehension Questions:

1. **(focus on word with phonics skill)** Find the word the author uses to describe the wolf. (*mean*) What does this tell you about the wolf?

2. **(detail with text evidence)** What did each pig use to make its home? Find the sentences that tell you this. How did this create, or make, a dilemma for each pig?

3. **(higher-level question)** Why wouldn't the pigs let the wolf in their homes?

4. **(higher-level question)** The man said, "Logs are best" for making a home. Do you agree? Why or why not?

5. **(connect to children's lives)** What are homes made of where we live?

Writing Prompt: Write a retelling of the story.

Fluency Plan: Have children reread the story to a partner on the following day. On a later day, have them reread the story to find (circle or list) words with *-ead, -eat, -eet,* and *-ee.*

Root for the Team (page 111)

Focus Phonics Skill: Long *oo*

Decodable Words With Phonics Skill: *boom, boot, noon, root, scoop, shoot, soon, zoom*

New High-Frequency and Story Words: *first, together*

BEFORE READING

Academic Vocabulary Word About the Book: *cooperate*

- **Define:** work together

- **Example:** We have to cooperate, or work together, to build the new playground.

- **Ask:** How do you cooperate with other people?

English-Learner Supports (e.g., vocabulary to preteach): *noon, root, players, coach, scream, field, scoop up, pass the ball, lean, far*

DURING READING

Technique (choral read, echo read, whisper read): Echo-read the first reading, modeling how to read sentences ending with exclamation points with greater enthusiasm. Then choral-read the second reading.

AFTER READING

Comprehension Questions:

1. **(focus on word with phonics skill)** What time will the team meet to practice? (*noon*) Find the word.

2. **(detail with text evidence)** How does the coach help the team? Find sentences that support your answer.

3. **(higher-level question)** Why does the team practice so much and so hard?

4. **(higher-level question)** Why does the coach say the soccer players are a "good team"?

5. **(connect to children's lives)** What teams have you played on? How did you and your teammates have to cooperate?

Writing Prompt: Make a list of the things the team did to prepare, or get ready, for the soccer game. Draw a picture to illustrate your list.

Fluency Plan: Have children reread the story to a partner on the following day. On a later day, have them reread the story to find (circle or list) words with *-oon* and *-oom*.

All Around the Farm (page 119)

Focus Phonics Skill: Diphthongs *ou, ow*

Decodable Words With Phonics Skill: *out, about, around, ground, house, round, sprouts, brown, down, how, now*

New High-Frequency and Story Words: *every, near*

BEFORE READING

Academic Vocabulary Word About the Book: *cultivate*

- **Define:** to grow
- **Example:** The farmer will cultivate the plants in his field.
- **Ask:** What does a farmer need to do to cultivate, or grow, plants?

English-Learner Supports (e.g., vocabulary to preteach): *farm, farmer, field, ground, yummy, ears of corn, seeds, sprouts, deep, ripe*

DURING READING

Technique (choral read, echo read, whisper read): Have children whisper-read the story while you listen in and offer feedback. Then echo-read, modeling how to change your intonation for sentences that end in a question mark or an exclamation point.

AFTER READING

Comprehension Questions:

1. **(focus on word with phonics skill)** Find the word that tells where Farmer Steve puts the seeds. (*ground*) What other words are used to name or describe the ground?

2. **(detail with text evidence)** What happens to the corn in the shed? Find the sentence that supports your answer.

3. **(higher-level question)** What are the steps in growing corn—from seed to table or store?

4. **(higher-level question)** What machines does Farmer Steve use? Why does he need them?

5. **(connect to students' lives)** What food plants have you grown or seen growing?

Writing Prompt: Write and draw the steps from planting a seed to having the food on your table to eat.

Fluency Plan: Have children reread the story to a partner on the following day. On a later day, have them reread the story to find (circle or list) words with *-own* and *-ound*.

DECODABLE MINI-BOOKS

Reproduce and assemble the following decodable mini-books to use with your students. (See page 127 for instructions on how to photocopy and assemble mini-books.)

- **Let's Grow Them** (page 87)
- **No Fun for Gus!** (page 95)
- **The Three Little Pigs** (page 103)
- **Root for the Team** (page 111)
- **All Around the Farm** (page 119)

These mini-books, along with several other decodable readers, are also available in full-color, small-group sets from Scholastic. Below is a complete list of the books and skills covered in Scholastic's *Phonics First Little Readers* library.

1. **I Like the ABCs** (alphabet)

2. **Dad** (short *a*)

3. **A Lot on Top** (short *o*)

4. **Will It Fit?** (short *i*)

5. **My Cat Can** (short *a* and short *o*)

6. **Who Has a Bill?** (short *a* and short *i*)

7. **Let's Grow Them** (short *e*)

8. **Max's Pet** (short vowels *a, e, i, o*)

9. **No Fun for Gus!** (short *u*)

10. **Shhh!** (short vowels and consonant digraphs)

11. **The Pancake Man** (final *e, a_e*)

12. **Hen Pen's Joke** (final *e, a_e, i_e, o_e, u_e*)

13. **The Three Little Pigs** (long *e*)

14. **Play the Animal Game!** (consonant blends)

15. **Say It and Smile!** (consonant blends)

16. **Whale of a Joke!** (consonant digraphs)

17. **The Frog Trail** (long *a*)

18. **Dinosaur Hall** (*au, aw, all*)

19. **Follow It!** (long *o*)

20. **The Hungry Toad** (more long *o*)

21. **Pizza Cook** (short *oo*)

22. **Root for the Team** (long *oo*)

23. **All Around the Farm** (diphthongs *ou, ow*)

24. **I Spy** (long *i*)

Let's Grow Them

by Nancy Leber and Amy Levin

My Words

are	and	in
grow	big	sit
let's	can	will
yes	dig	
you		

-en

Ben
ten

-et

get
wet

italics = new high-frequency and story words

"What's that?" said Jess.

"Ten  seeds," said Ben.

Cut along dotted line.

See the big, red tomatoes.

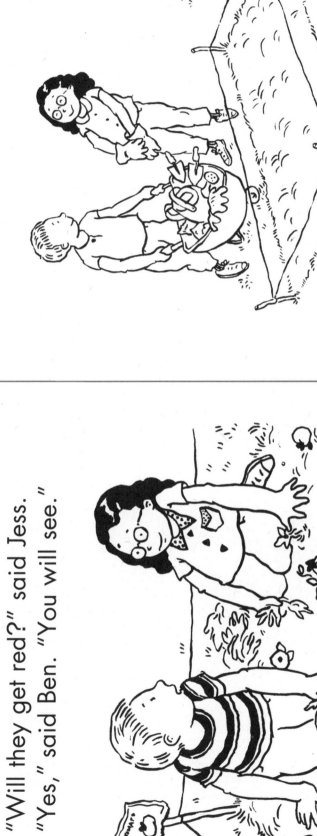

"Let's grow them," said Ben.

Choosing and Using Decodable Texts © 2021 by Wiley Blevins, Scholastic Inc.

"Will they get red?" said Jess.
"Yes," said Ben. "You will see."

14

4

Ben and Jess dig and dig and
dig and dig.

Choosing and Using Decodable Texts © 2021 by Wiley Blevins, Scholastic Inc.

13

"They will get big," said Ben.

The  seeds are in!

"Will they get big?" said Jess.

12

Ben gets a can.

Jess gets a  hose .

Cut along dotted line.

"They will grow," said Ben.

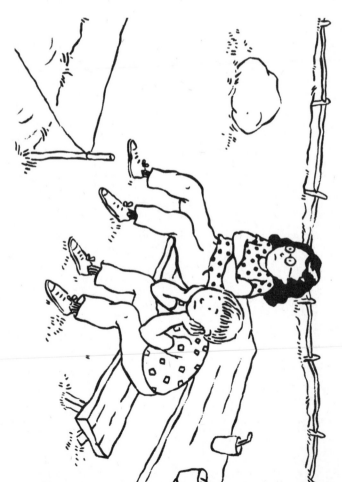

Choosing and Using Decodable Texts © 2021 by Wiley Blevins, Scholastic Inc.

The get wet.
seeds

"Will the grow?" said Jess.
seeds

Choosing and Using Decodable Texts © 2021 by Wiley Blevins, Scholastic Inc.

10

93

Ben and Jess sit and sit.

They sit and sit.

Cut along dotted line.

No Fun for Gus!

by Nancy Leber and Amy Levin

Cut along dotted line.

My Words

his	bit	got
missed	cap	had
then	Dad	in
and	fell	leg
at	get	on
Uu	**-ub**	**-ug**
mud	tub	bug
stuck	**-um**	**-un**
	drum	bun
	gum	fun
		-us
		bus
		Gus

italics = new high-frequency and story words

Choosing and Using Decodable Texts © 2021 by Wiley Blevins, Scholastic Inc.

"This is no fun," said Gus.
Gus missed the bus.

Cut along dotted line.

Choosing and Using Decodable Texts © 2021 by Wiley Blevins, Scholastic Inc.

"This is fun!" said Gus.
Brumm! Brumm! Brumm!

His bun fell at lunch.
"This is no fun," said Gus.

"The drum!" said Dad and Gus.

Choosing and Using Decodable Texts © 2021 by Wiley Blevins, Scholastic Inc.

"This is no fun," said Gus.
A bug bit his leg.

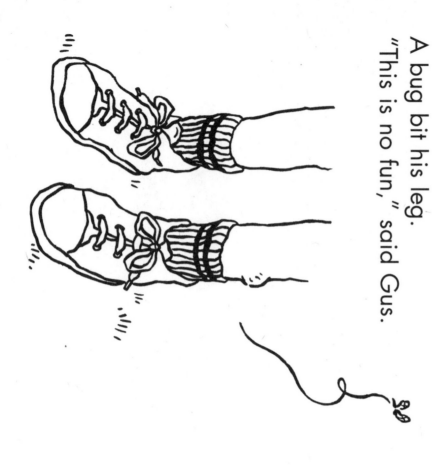

Cut along dotted line.

"Ummm,"
said Gus.

"Ummm,"
said Dad.

Gum got stuck on his cap.
"This is no fun," said Gus.

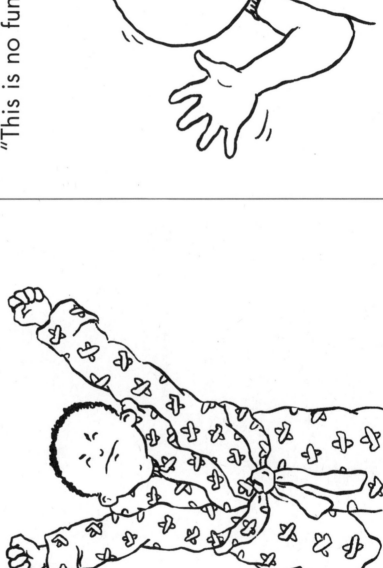

5

Cut along dotted line.

Choosing and Using Decodable Texts © 2021 by Wiley Blevins, Scholastic Inc.

"WHERE IS MY DRUM?" said Gus.

12

9

Then Gus fell in the mud.
"This is no fun," said Gus.

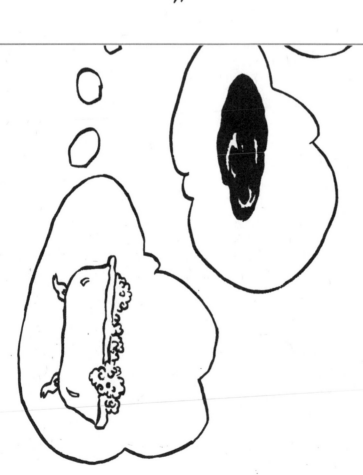

Cut along dotted line.

"I fell in the mud.
Then I had to get in the tub."

11

"Get in the tub," said his dad.
"This is no fun," said Gus.

"A bug bit my leg.
Gum got stuck on my cap."

8

"Where is my drum?"
"THIS IS NO FUN!" said Gus.

6

"I missed the bus.
My bun fell at lunch."

Choosing and Using Decodable Texts © 2021 by Wiley Blevins, Scholastic Inc.

The Three Little Pigs

a retelling by Gail Tuchman

My Words

away   I'll   one   over   toes

ea	**ee**	**-eat**
leaped	feet	eat
mean	free	heat
please	see	
read	sleep	
	three	

Story Words: blow, chimney, Wolf

italics = new high-frequency and story words

Choosing and Using Decodable Texts © 2021 by Wiley Blevins, Scholastic Inc.

Three little pigs set out to see the land. Pig One met a man with cut grass and said, "Please sell me some grass to make a home."

Cut along dotted line.

But Mean Wolf leaped out and ran free. He did not come back for the little pigs three.

Yikes!

Choosing and Using Decodable Texts © 2021 by Wiley Blevins, Scholastic Inc.

3

"Grass won't work," said the man.
But Pig One made a home of grass
where he could sleep.

Choosing and Using Decodable Texts © 2021 by Wiley Blevins, Scholastic Inc.

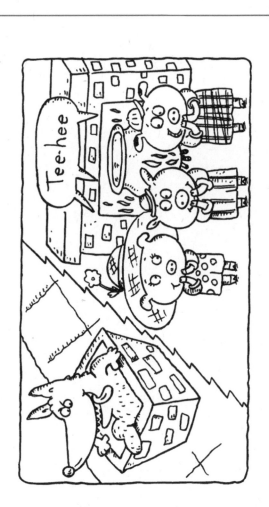

Tee-hee

"Here I come down the chimney,"
he yelled. "It's time to eat."
"Yes, it is," said the pigs as they
put a big pot on the flames.

14

Mean Wolf came by. He said, "Little pig, let me in from the heat." "No," said the pig. "Not by the toes on my feet, feet, feet."

He huffed and puffed but he could not blow the home down. Mean Wolf was mad!

Huff

Puff

Choosing and Using Decodable Texts © 2021 by Wiley Blevins, Scholastic Inc.

"Then I'll huff and I'll puff and I'll blow your home down," said Mean Wolf. So he did and the pig ran away.

Cut along dotted line.

Mean Wolf came by and said, "Little pigs, let me in from the heat." "No," said the pigs. "Not by the toes on our feet, feet, feet."

6

Pig Two met a woman with sticks and said, "Please sell me some sticks to make a home."

"Sticks won't work," she said.

Cut along dotted line.

11

Pig Three made a home of logs where she could eat and read and sleep. Pigs One and Two came over.

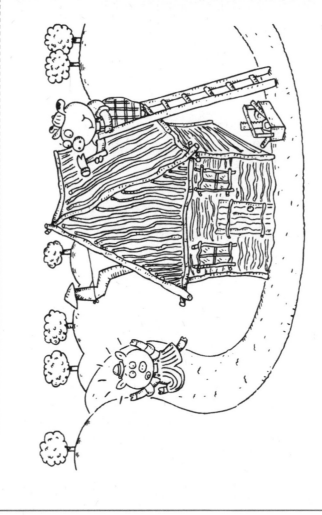

But Pig Two made a home of sticks where he could eat and sleep. Pig One came running in.

Cut along dotted line.

Pig Three met a man with logs and said, "Please sell me some logs to make a home."

"Logs are best!" the man said.

8

Mean Wolf came over and said,
"Little pigs, let me in from the heat."
"No," said the pigs. "Not by the
toes on our feet, feet, feet."

"Then I'll huff and I'll puff and
I'll blow your home down," said
Mean Wolf. So he did and the pigs
ran away.

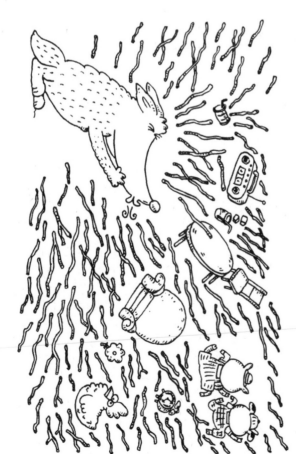

9

Choosing and Using Decodable Texts © 2021 by Wiley Blevins, Scholastic Inc.

Root for the Team

by Nancy Leber

My Words

first together

oo

boom   scoop
boot   shoot
noon   soon
root   zoom

Story Words: Daniel, field, force, goalie, player, soccer

italics = new high-frequency and story words

Daniel is a soccer coach. He leads a team and tells the players what to do. The team will meet at noon.

Meet the Team

Cut along dotted line.

"You worked together," says the coach. "Now you are a good team!"
"Hooray!" screams the team.

The players on the team come to the field. 1, 2, 3, 4, 5, 6, 7, 8, 9, 10, 11. The Strike Force is here.

3

Soon the Strike Force is near the goal. They scoop up the ball, but the other team is in the way. The ball gets in! The coach roots for his team.

14

Cut along dotted line.

The coach wants the team to play well. "Let's work together and soon we will be a good team," he says.

Cut along dotted line.

The Strike Force goalie kicks the ball back to his team. The players pass the ball to each other. "Boot the ball!" calls the coach.

Choosing and Using Decodable Texts © 2021 by Wiley Blevins, Scholastic Inc.

The Team Drills

It is time to drill. "If you are not close to your team, make a long kick," says the coach. "Come see." Boom! He kicks the ball.

Cut along dotted line.

The teams run to the ball. The Strike Force gets to it first and kicks. Then the other team gets to it and shoots.

Now the team works on long kicks.
"When you kick, put your toes down," says the coach.

Now it is time for the game.
The two teams line up for the kickoff.
The coach talks to his players from the sideline.

The Game

Choosing and Using Decodable Texts © 2021 by Wiley Blevins, Scholastic Inc.

Jane runs to the ball.
Boom! She kicks it.
Z-o-o-m! It goes far!

The players do the chip shots
over and over. "Let's work together
and soon we will be a good team!"
the coach calls out.

Choosing and Using Decodable Texts © 2021 by Wiley Blevins, Scholastic Inc.

"Here is a way to shoot if a player is in your way," says the coach. He shows the team how to make a chip shot.

8

"Scoop up the ball like this when you kick." The coach leans back and slips his toes under the ball.

9

Cut along dotted line.

All Around the Farm

by Amy Levin

My Words

every   near

ou

out
about
around
ground

house
round
sprouts

ow

brown
down
how
now

Story Words: California, corn, farm, farmer, machine

italics = new high-frequency and story words

Choosing and Using Decodable Texts © 2021 by Wiley Blevins, Scholastic Inc.

Steve is a farmer. Steve grows
corn on a farm in California.
He likes life on the farm.

Cut along dotted line.

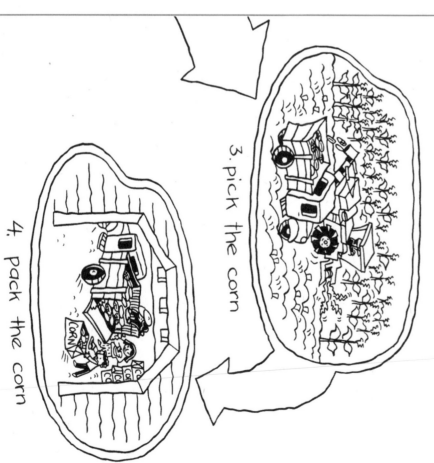

3. pick the corn

4. pack the corn

Choosing and Using Decodable Texts © 2021 by Wiley Blevins, Scholastic Inc.

Steve rises before the sun comes up and goes out to the fields. There is a lot to do every day on a farm.

3

How does the corn get from the farm to your house?

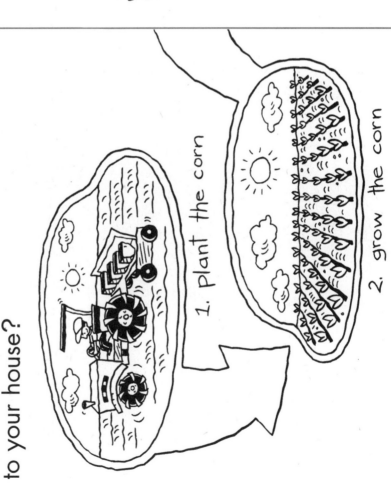

1. Plant the corn

2. grow the corn

14

He bends down to feel the rich brown ground. The sun is up now, and it feels hot on his back. It's a good day to plant some corn!

When the sun goes down, it's time for a yummy farm meal. There is meat, beets, beans, and lots of corn!

Cut along dotted line.

Choosing and Using Decodable Texts © 2021 by Wiley Blevins, Scholastic Inc.

Cut along dotted line.

Steve uses a machine to help him.
It drops each seed into the ground.
A wheel packs the seeds down deep.

5

Then Steve puts each box on a big truck. This truck will take the corn to places near and far.

12

The corn seeds need a lot of sun and water. Soon sprouts will come out. Then the corn will grow until it is very tall.

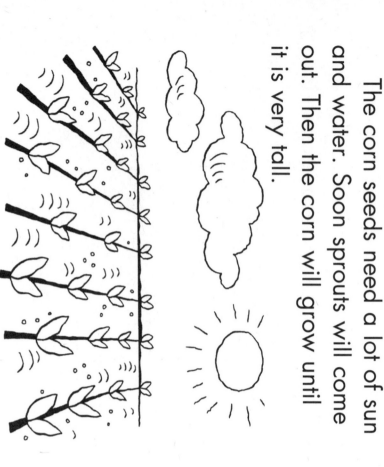

Big and little ears of corn fill a truck! The truck takes them to a shed where the corn is packed in boxes.

Cut along dotted line.

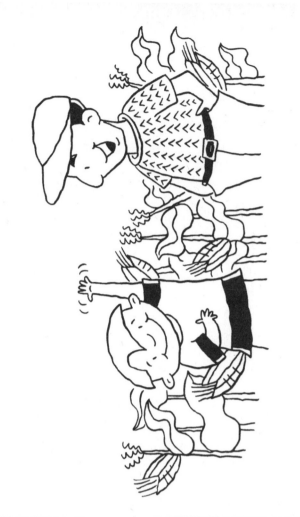

Look how tall it is now! Steve will teach his son about growing corn. One day his son can help him.

Choosing and Using Decodable Texts © 2021 by Wiley Blevins, Scholastic Inc.

Steve uses a big machine to pick the corn. It goes up and down the tall fields, picking corn along the way.

Now Steve wants to see if the corn is ripe. He rips off an ear of corn to take a look at it.

8

He peels back the thick green husk. The corn inside is round and yellow. It is ready to pick!

9

Choosing and Using Decodable Texts © 2021 by Wiley Blevins, Scholastic Inc.

How to Make the Mini-Books

Follow these steps to copy and assemble the mini-books:

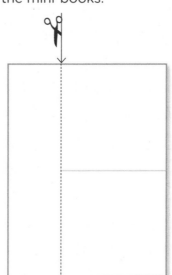

1. Remove the book pages. (You can also download PDF versions online; see page 5 for information on how to access.) Make double-sided copies on 8½-by-11-inch paper. Cut along the dashed line.

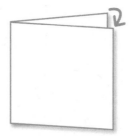

2. Fold each page along the center line.

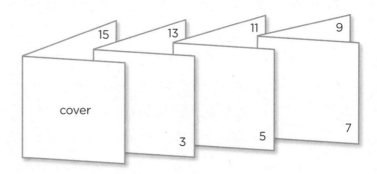

3. Place the pages in order, starting with the cover.

cover

15 13 11 9

3 5 7

4. Staple the pages along the book's spine.

SELECT REFERENCES

Adams, M. J. (1990). *Beginning to read: Thinking and learning about print*. Cambridge, MA: Massachusetts Institute of Technology.

Anderson, R. C., Hiebert, E. H., Scott, J. A., & Wilkinson, I. A. G. (1985). *Becoming a nation of readers: The report of the Commission on Reading*. Champaign, IL: Center for the Study of Reading and National Academy of Education.

Blevins, W. (2020). *Meaningful phonics and word study: Lesson fix ups for impactful teaching*. New Rochelle, NY: Benchmark Education.

Blevins, W. (2019). Meeting the challenges of early literacy phonics instruction. *Literacy leadership brief* No. 9452. International Literacy Association.

Blevins, W. (2016). *A fresh look at phonics: Common causes of failure and 7 ingredients for success*. Thousand Oaks, CA: Corwin.

Blevins, W. (2017a). *Phonics from A to Z: A practical guide. 3rd edition*. New York, NY: Scholastic.

Blevins, W. (2017b). *Teaching phonics and word study in the intermediate grades. 2nd edition*. New York, NY: Scholastic.

Blevins, W. (2011a). *Teaching the alphabet: A flexible, systematic approach to building early phonics skills*. New York, NY: Scholastic.

Blevins, W. (2011b). *Teaching phonics: A flexible, systematic approach to building early reading skills*. New York, NY: Scholastic.

Blevins, W. (2011c). *Week-by-week phonics and word study activities for the intermediate grades*. New York, NY: Scholastic.

Cheatham, J. P. & Allor, J. H. (2012). The influence of decodability in early reading text on reading achievement: A review of the evidence. *Reading and writing: An interdisciplinary journal, 25*(9), 2223–2246.

Chu, M. & Chen, S. (2014). Comparison of the effects of two phonics training programs on L2 word reading. *Psychological reports, 114*(1), 272–291. https://doi.org/10.2466/28.10.pr0.114k17w0.

Frey, R. C. (2012). *Rethinking the role of decodable texts in early literacy instruction*. (UMI No. 3593795) [Doctoral dissertation, University of California, Berkeley]. ProQuest Dissertations Publishing. https://www.proquest.com/docview/1441347886

Gough, P. and Tunmer, W. (1986). Decoding, reading, and reading disability. *Remedial and special education, 7*, 6–10.

Hoffman, J. V., Sailors, M., & Patterson, E. U. (2002). Decodable texts for beginning reading instruction: The year 2000 basals. *Journal of literacy research, 34*(3), pp. 269–298. doi:10.1207/s15548430jlr3403_2

Jenkins, J. R., Peyton, J. A., Sanders, E. A., & Vadasy, P. F. (2004). Effects of reading decodable texts in supplemental first-grade tutoring. *Scientific studies of reading, 8*(1), 53–85, https://doi.org/10.1207/s1532799xssr0801_4

Juel, C., & Roper-Schneider, D. (1985). The influence of basal readers on first-grade reading. *Reading research quarterly, 20*(2), 134–152. https://doi.org/10.2307/747751

Mesmer, H. A. E. (2005). Text decodability and the first-grade reader. *Reading & writing quarterly 21*(1). 61–86.

National Institute of Child Health and Human Development. (2000). *Report of the National Reading Panel: Teaching children to read: An evidence-based assessment of the scientific literature on reading and its implications for reading instruction*. (NIH Publication No. 00–4769). Washington, DC: U.S. Government Printing Office.

Rasinski, T. V. (2005). *Daily word ladders*. New York, NY: Scholastic.

Scarborough, H. S. (2001). Connecting early language and literacy to later reading (dis)abilities: Evidence, theory, and practice. In S. Neuman & D. Dickinson (Eds.), *Handbook for research in early literacy* (pp. 97–110). New York, NY: Guilford Press.

Schwartz, S. (2020). Decodable books: Boring, useful, or both? *Education week, 39*(26), 1, 15.

Stein, M., Johnson, B. & Gutlohn, L. (1999). Analyzing beginning reading programs: The relationship between decoding instruction and text. *Remedial and special education, 20*(5). 275–287. doi:10.1177/074193259902000503

Wong, M. (2015, May 29). Brain wave study shows how different teaching methods affect reading development. *Psychology & psychiatry*. Medical Xpress. Retrieved from medicalxpress.com/news/2015-05-brain-methods-affect.html